Respects of the author to
Father Gallagher

Vincent Mc Crossen

THE NEW RENAISSANCE OF THE SPIRIT

THE NEW RENAISSANCE OF THE SPIRIT

BY

VINCENT A. McCROSSEN

Professor of Modern Languages
Marietta College, Marietta, Ohio

PHILOSOPHICAL LIBRARY
NEW YORK

AD MARIAM MEDIATRICEM

PREFACE AND ACKNOWLEDGMENT

THE BOOK REPRESENTS the author's reaction to his studies in comparative literature and thought in some thirty languages which cover a span of over three thousand years of Western civilization. The privilege of studying and teaching the great inspirational thought of many centuries brings with it the responsibility of interpreting the pertinency of our culture to any age, including our own. Many of the most serious thinkers of our time have grappled with the problem of the seeming disintegration of the modern world. This book reviews the forces conflicting for supremacy in our age. Out of this conflict it sees a new hope for Western civilization renewed on a spiritual basis. It suggests that new and daring solutions are called for in order for modern man to rebuild his world upon the only values on which a great civilization can rest—the attributes of God: Truth, Beauty, Justice, Mercy, Creativity, Faith, Hope, Love. After a century of despair and frustration and decadence as the dominant notes of literature, *The New Renaissance of the Spirit,* at the same time that it emphasizes the solemn and alarming seriousness of the pangs of parturition of our new age, sounds a new and daring peal of challenge and hope and faith at our tottering world.

Grateful acknowledgment is made by the author to

the Most Reverend John T. McNicholas, Archbishop of Cincinnati and Chairman of the Administrative Board of the National Catholic Welfare Conference, to the Most Reverend John King Mussio, Bishop of Steubenville, and to the Knights of Columbus, Steubenville, Ohio for their help and encouragement of the author in his work.

CONTENTS

ix

CONTENTS

CHAPTER ONE

THE NATURE OF OUR NEW RENAISSANCE

Dawn of a new world

"And there was a certain rich man who was clothed in purple and fine linen and feasted sumptuously every day. And there was a certain beggar named Lazarus, who lay at his gate full of sores, desiring to be filled with the crumbs that fell from the rich man's table . . . . And it came to pass that the beggar died and was carried by the angels into Abraham's bosom; and the rich man also died, and he was buried in Hell. And lifting up his eyes when he was in torments, he saw Abraham afar off and Lazarus in his bosom . . . . And he cried: 'Father Abraham, I beseech thee, send him to my father's house that he may testify unto them, lest they come into this place of torments.' And Abraham said to him: 'They have Moses and the prophets: let them hear them.' But he said: 'No, Father Abraham! But if one went to them from the dead, they will do penance.' And He said to him: 'If they hear not Moses and the prophets, neither will they believe if one rise from the dead.' " Luke, XVI, 19-31.

THE SIMPLE STARTLING truth of Christ's parable is as valid in the crisis facing Western civilization today as it was in the turning point of Western civilization some nineteen hundred years ago when Christ made His statement. Man is blind to the needs of his time and obdurate in refusing to understand its nature. As in the time of Christ, men of today frequently would not believe even if someone should rise from the dead to tell them what must be done. The Roman Empire of Christ's time did not believe Him even when He rose from the dead, did not accept His admonitions and His teachings that it should abandon its

I

materialistic and pragmatic tests of value, did not comprehend the forces of spirituality which He set in motion in the world; and because it did not believe and did not comprehend, it became an historical memory. And unless modern civilization believes the admonitions and principles of Christ and unless it comprehends the forces in motion in its time, it shall likewise perish.

Our blindness is even more appalling than that of ancient Rome. We have not only Christ risen from the dead to believe. We have a whole world risen from the dead to give us warning. We have the mirror and fateful example of the ancient Roman mother ever before us to give us testimony and to cry out to the modern world, to the new, resurrected Rome so like unto the old, the directions in which lie the paths of ruin and of dissolution. Yet, the modern world does not believe either its God risen from the dead or the lessons shouted at it from its ancient prototype, lessons which bear witness from the dead that those cultures whose hierarchy of values and criteria of truth are rooted in the senses, in materialism and pragmatism, in the primacy of terrestrial existence, shall perish.

The twentieth century A. D., like the first century A. D., is a transition period between two worlds, between the imposing, impressive pagan and materialistic and utilitarian past and the glorious, idealistic spiritual, and religious future. Just as truly as in the first century A. D. forces were already at work replacing the tired and weary, even sated, civilization of Rome with a youthful, exuberant, confident civilization of Europe, replacing the old values of material possessions and power and security by new values of the spirit, of the uplift of the mind and soul to God, of eternity and man's place in it, so in our time similar forces are at work replacing our centuries old tests of value in the primacy of life and possessions and the abundant sensate world by tests of value in terms of God, of the spirit, of eternity, in terms of the infinite relationship between God and man. We are in a new Renaissance of the Spirit just as ineluctably as was the Rome of Christ and Peter and Paul, of Augustus and Tiberius.

A new world dawns before us more exciting, more challenging than any world out of the past has even been. It is a world far newer and with far greater hope than even the New World which once Columbus gave to the eager desires and hopes and aspirations of his wearying continent. The voyages of discovery and conquest and winning of this new world dwarf into insignificance the feeble gropings of the past, of Balboa and De Soto and Hudson, of Da Gama and Magellan and Marquette, of Clark and Lewis. For Columbus opened only a new hemisphere for development and expansion, for the birth of mere new nations and new empires. Modern man has extended before him an entire new world. The old New World, which Columbus opened, was only a world for man, to be developed by the exploitation and passion and greed, and for the profit and selfishness of man. But the new world which dawns today is a world of God, with man under the Fatherhood of God, recognizing and obeying Him, loving and knowing and serving Him as man has not known God for centuries past, perhaps loving and knowing and serving Him better than man has ever loved and known and served his God before.

It is a world of the Brotherhood of man. It is a world which, if it is to be born with minimal travail, needs the best intellects and imagination and genius and prayers and faith of man, needs them more than any age past has ever needed them. Our time is in *infinite* needs of these things— and of the help of God. We are, indeed, in many respects

3

at the dawn of our new age as very little children. We are rich with almost endless potentiality. We can rightly be exuberant with enthusiasm at the future before us. But we need also the caution and help of our Creator Parent, unless the new world is to come upon us only through untold misery and suffering and chaos. In all the enthusiasm and exuberance of our youth we need the steadying hand of God as no age past has ever needed it. One of the great tragedies of our time can be that modern man, relying blindly only on himself and on his past, remains unconscious both of the future which dawns before him and of his own helplessness. without God. The future would then still remain to us, but the path into it would almost certainly be one fraught with hellish frightfulness. Our attitude toward our future should be one of endless optimism, but at the same time an optimism steadied by caution and inspired by prayer.

We are at the cross roads between a dying order and one coming to birth. In the world that is passing the driving force has been pursuit of self-interest, of wealth and power, of comfort and security. It has been a devil-take-the-hindmost competition, often without thought that the comfort and security and wealth after which the members of society sought with might and main were often gained at the expense of the comfort and security and well being of other members of the social order. It has been a world unpermeated by Love of God, almost always with only lip service to God; and frequently in its gathering contemporary totalitarian horrors, it has been even without such lip service, a world marked by the downright negation of God. It has been a world with a minimal sense of duty and justice and responsibility and cohesion upon the part of the members of the social order toward one another and within the various social groups toward other social groups. There has been just enough sense of duty and responsibility and coöperation and justice to avoid the worst universal explosions which would upheave the material order irremediably. Even so, the explosions which have resulted from the lack of adequate justice and coöperation and duty and responsibility are coming ever closer to shatter the material order at its foundations, so that modern man has sober need to wonder if there is a-work in his present society even such minimal justice and coöperation to avoid a world wide irremediable shattering.

The chief rewards of the past have gone to those who owned or controlled the means of production. The possessors of property and industry have often looked upon the state and its inhabitants as tools to be used for the aggrandizement of their wealth and power and influence. True, they have often looked upon the members of society as worthy tools and have frequently treated them well, sharing with them a part of their gains and affording them a modicum of justice because their human tools had served them well. More recently, totalitarian horrors mixing monstrous evil with minimal good have set restraints upon the limits of self-interest and self-gain, but in doing so have established a tyranny over the human tool, enslaving him under the mighty hand of the state, so as to rob him of even the vestiges of dignity and decency and divine worth. They have bestialized him, mechanized him, rendered him into complete machine, denying him his soul and his sonship before God. The philosophy of the old dying world has been materialistic, whether a materialism mixed with a minimum of lip service to God and His laws and order, or the complete, shameless, godless materialism of the more recent totalitarian horrors.

5

In the society that is dawning the common good will be supreme, not merely the materialistic "common good" mouthed by our dictators and misleaders of the people, a will-o'-the-wisp dangled forth to those thirsting for justice to keep in power those who are often a mockery of justice. Rather, the order of the new world will be a common good under God. The common good under God will protect many values which the totalitarian "common good" of our time has either ignored or openly and shamelessly assailed. The common good under God must promote the welfare and rights and sacredness of the individual. For unless the individual is safe, the common good is an illusion. The common good is really the accumulative individual good. The common good must protect the family as the basis of all society. The common good under God must protect the right of the individual and of the family to private property rightfully and honestly acquired. Yet, it must not place property rights before human rights. Totalitarianism, both of the right and of the left, in our time has given only the slightest inkling of what is meant by such common good. Totalitarianism in a certain sense has been an awkward groping step into the future to the degree that it has laid restraint upon unbridled individualism riding rough-shod over the members of the social order. It has emphasized that individual selfishness can wreck the social order and hence needs to be restrained. Yet, totalitarianism has not been a cure, but a worse disease than the first. It has assaulted the individual, the family, and private property. Without a sense of law and justice and a power higher than itself, it has bestialized man and enslaved him. It has denied and flouted the absolute power of God, and substituted the myth of the community, the state, as the source of all right and wrong.

It has substituted a part of creation for the Creator and bidden man worship it. It has mouthed platitudes about "common good" and wrought monstrous evil both to the community and to the individual. That totalitarianism has brought into focus some of the evil of the unbridled self-interest of the past is undeniable. That it is a proper order is slanderous nonsense.

The dawning world must reconstruct the social order, but it must do it under the Love of God, not under the bestializing tyranny of men. Men in the new world must be bound together by a new sense of duty and responsibility, such as has not existed in Western civilization since the best days of the feudal system. Man must become the brother and keeper of his fellow man. Everything that concerns his brother concerns him. What is done for the mightiest must be done also for the least.

The gifts of God were not meant to be pursued to the exclusion of the Giver. Past man has worshipped and desired the gift. He has often ignored the Giver. He has almost never loved Him a pittance of His due. Past man has made the world all topsy-turvy, shaken it out of all due order and proportion in pursuing the gift and failing to know and honor and love the Giver. But the gaze of future man must be directed first to the Giver of all good gifts. With his vision directed toward his Creator, future man can understand that the gifts of God have been made for all men and all nations and all races to share in. The energies that once man misdirected to competing with and outstripping his fellows, trampling over them, combatting them in the fury for getting and having and enjoying, for holding on to and yet ever seizing more, he can direct toward building the most proper society that has ever existed, a society knowing and serving and loving God.

7

Underlying the new world must be the concept that human personality, not in and by itself, but human personality because it is created by God and created for an eternity with Him, is of infinite worth. Man must be free —for God. Liberty in spite of the thundering crash of totalitarian tyranny around us must be preserved to hold open the way to equality and fraternity, not the mere vapid, empty, meaningless materialistic equality and fraternity of the French Revolution run amuck, but of equality and fraternity under God.

The challenge made to modern man is one of the greatest and most terrifying challenges which has ever been put to him since his fall from grace in Eden, unquestionably the greatest challenge made to him since his God, Incarnate Man, walked in his midst on earth, ministered unto him, and sought his loving acknowledgement. The question is how soon and how well, or how belatedly and how blindly, will modern man accept the challenge flung to him? How wisely or how stupidly will he help the new world into birth?

Too few people in the Western world at the present moment really understand the nature of our time and the New Renaissance, really comprehend the forces at work in it. Countless numbers vaguely and uncomfortably are sensing the forces astir without comprehending them. Such individuals are alert enough to feel that one world is dying, but are not keen enough to know that another is being born and still less to grasp what type of world is springing to birth to replace the old, outmoded one. Their malaise and discomfort stem from belonging completely neither to the world of the past and the dying present nor to the dawning future. They are the "expressionists" of forces they cannot comprehend in expressing but which they so inescapably feel that they cannot silence them.

The simple truth is that the world is in the midst of a vast shift of values away from those of the past into those of the future, a vast cleavage in philosophies, in standards of truth, in criteria and hierarchies of value. Because this cleavage is scarcely understood at all, modern men are bewildered, confused, sensing only that there is upheaval. They do not examine and frequently are unwilling to examine the nature of their New Renaissance. They are unwilling to admit the testimony of their own senses that the world of the past is literally dissolving about them. They are instinctively afraid of change; and only when the reality of the upheaval forces itself in physical frightfulness upon them are they jarred into some groping comprehension of the volcanic nature of their time. Even then they frequently see only its physical horror and not its long range trend. If such unwillingness to examine the cleavage in the hierarchy of values and such blindness in comprehending the nature of the upheaval of our time persist, they can have only the most tragic results, prolonging the chaos and the disruption of the transition from one type of world to the other, marring the future, and extending the misery and death agony of the world of the past into a needlessly wretched and needlessly lengthy present. Modern man must examine his own tests of value, those of his dying past, and those of his dawning future to comprehend the forces fermenting in his own day and to live and work intelligently and creatively in his New Renaissance. He must divest himself of his complacency and stagnation if the alternative is not to be universal jarring of terrible and awful physical frightfulness.

For we are ankle-deep in our new Renaissance. By the

9

end of the century we shall be in it up to the knees, whether we like it or not. We can no more halt our future than we can arrest a volcano in eruption or stay the quaking of the earth. Willy-nilly, *volentes nolentes* we shall be carried forward by our time. However, we shall not be its puppets. For the greatest, the most responsible, the most terrifying gift which God has given man is free will. Free will gives man a choice among courses of action. With free will man is not forced by the times or the environment or heredity or glands into a superimposed or inevitable course of action. Man is not enslaved by forces beyond his control. He is free to make a choice, to act rightly or to act wrongly. He is given the grace to make correct choices. But he is not *forced* to put such grace into efficacious action. He can reject and nullify his grace, or he can accept it and implement it. And he is responsible for his choice, responsible in terms of both good and evil, of reward and punishment. Free will is an ennobling gift but a terrifying one. It is basic to man's freedom and to his dignity. But it gives him a responsibility both to himself and to others, the effect of which may endure for centuries.

Our twentieth century is a time of staggering responsibility, a period of transition between two completely opposite forms of civilization. Our free will determines the nature and the length of the transition. Our free will, while it will not entirely and exclusively shape the future, will, at least, control it, determine it, establish how disruptive, how chaotic, how volcanic the transition from the past into the future shall or shall not be. The ways in which we *will* to act will mark the severity or the gentleness of the transition and will leave their impress on the next five hundred—or, perhaps, the next thousand years. Our sins of commission, and, perchance, more important still, our sins of omission, will in their effects be visited upon our children for generations. And if our good works and our virtues outweigh our committed and omitted deleterious acts, our children for equal generations may in humility and peace, in justice and in hope be borne into their future which now so threateningly impends.

The Renaissance in which we now stand is the direct opposite in the tests of value which it will eventually establish of the Renaissance of seven hundred years ago. By tests of value are meant the things and ideas and concepts which men prize. Human beings regularly prize certain aspects of life more than others. Their prized aspects are their tests of value. If a man puts his faith in God, he may be said to have a spiritual test of value. If he puts his faith in wealth or power or the perishable things of earth, he may be said to have materialistic tests of value. Our New Renaissance is the birth of a new type of world, a world with new, spiritual tests of value.

It is also a rebirth, but in no sense a restoration, of the same type of world as the last Renaissance destroyed. The last Renaissance destroyed a spiritual world and ushered in the rebirth of the same type of materialistic world which had existed many centuries before in pagan Rome. The modern materialistic world, no matter how much akin it has been to Rome, has still been a new world, uniquely and wonderfully new. So it is also with our New Renaissance. It marks the destruction of the materialistic Roman-modern type of world of the past. It is a rebirth of the world of the spirit, the type of world temporarily destroyed by the past Renaissance. But the New Renaissance of the Spirit will not restore the medieval world, any more than our last Renaissance restored Rome. Our new world will be unique and different from any world which has ever been, no matter how much it may be a sister world in spirit to the Middle Ages. A Renaissance can never usher in a restoration of any past world. The past is dead, because the people and ideas, the physical mold which gave it form, are dead. Time does not ever put the new wine into the old and discarded containers. What the renaissances bring back are not the form and substance but the kindredship of nature. Renaissances are like mothers bearing different children, each child unique and different and pulsing with its own life, yet at the same time inheriting a common strain and marked by certain family resemblances. Different and unique, Rome and modernity were yet sisters. So also different and unique, the dawning world of the spirit will yet be a sister to the spiritual cultures which have gone before.

The most important thing to understand about a civilization is its hierarchy of values. With this clear all else about a civilization falls into pattern. If we know its tests of value, we can tell almost everything significant about the nature of a civilization. For its tests of value make its very soul, or the absence of its soul. They determine its life, its goals, its purposes. They permeate its culture. They are the theme of its books, its art, its monuments, its songs. They are frozen in its architecture and its sculpture. They are imprinted in its speech, its conversations. The tests of value of a culture motivate its members. They determine for them their morality or lack of morality, their standards of conduct, their ideals. They name the heroes of a culture. For the tests of value of a civilization are those tests by which the majority of its members live, work, and die. The members of a culture are dominated by them every day of their lives, every waking moment.

Even their dreams and visions are filled with the tests of value to which their civilization clings. Even the very manner of their dying, their last moments of life, are determined by their tests of value.

Sunset of the dying world of the senses

Western civilization has for its three to five thousand years of known historical existence revolved around two entirely contradictory sets of values. When one type of test of value has been in the ascendency, the other has been pushed into the background for many centuries. When one type has become weary, the other has replaced it, only to be replaced itself when its predecessor after a thousand years' rest has regained its strength and re-emerged into dominance. The sweep of western civilization is, therefore, not one unbroken curve upward as the nineteenth century evolutionist sometimes naïvely believed. It resembles rather the waves of the sea, each wave with its own crest and trough, its rising and swell, its ebbing and receding. There can be little talk of progress from one to the other type of civilization resting on different tests of value. Even the similarity to the succession of the waves of the sea may be misleading. For the stress is not on the rise and the fall. It is on difference and cleavage, on succession and change. We do not progress from one or regress into the other. We change our tests of value. Progress and regress are terms which appeal to those who do not grasp the real sweep of things, who are so rooted in one type of test of value that they do not catch the significance of the other. To them those civilizations which represent their own tests of value are periods of progress; those which do not are periods of regress or even "dark ages". Progress and regress are conveniently obfuscatory terms into which the closed mind can retreat in order to hide from itself the reality of the undulations in the hierarchy of values by which western man lives.

The world of the Hebrew prophets, of ancient Greece, of early Rome, and of the medieval period held to one type of test of values. The ancient Minoan culture, decadent Hellenistic Greece, megalopolitan Rome, and the modern world since the Renaissance of the thirteenth to the sixteenth centuries held to an entirely different set. We are now seeing this Cretan-Hellenistic-Roman-"modern" set yield again to the Hebrew-Homeric-medieval.

According to the Roman-modern type of tests of value —which we shall henceforth call sensate or materialistic or utilitarian or pagan, according to its overtone—those matters are good and true and valuable, and are, therefore, *recherchés,* which have to do with the immediacy of the everyday world and the primacy of life. The sensate tests of value concern principally things, objects, sensations, situations which contribute to man's physical happiness, enjoyment, comfort, and general well being. Sensate values are rooted in the here and the now, in the getting, the having, and the enjoying. They look upon life as an end in itself. Those who cling to sensate values make it their purpose to spend their life getting and having and enjoying as much as possible life's great treasures, living the "richest" life possible. Such sensate living is not at all necessarily limited to the slogan of "eat, drink and be merry, for tomorrow we die", of *"carpe diem"*, of *"cueillez,, cueillez votre jeunesse"*. At their lower levels sensate values may, of course, be rather exclusively animalistic and sensuous, looking little further than wine, women, and song, a well-fed and housed digestive system, animalistic security and comfort. But they run through the gamut of all sensate living to the highest aesthetic and cultured enjoyment for their own sake of the best which has been said and thought and conceived and drawn and written.

At the higher levels sensate values can without over much straining become spiritual values. But the dividing line is never tenuous or obscure. As long as the value is rooted in the primacy of life and of the senses and is enjoyed solely for its own sake, it remains a sensate value. When the result becomes the uplift of the individual, the ennobling and growth of his spirit, a bringing of him closer to God, it becomes a spiritual value. Thus, the same experience might present two different values to two different individuals, even to the same individual at different times The enjoyment of great music or of a great book or painting, if it brings delight only to the senses and is sought only for its own sake, remains a sensate value, albeit a very high one. But if it brings an individual peace and calm, cleanses his mind and spirit, gives him clearer understanding, results in some of that *katharsis* for which the Greeks had such deep comprehension, or, best of all, makes some segment of God's truth or God's great gifts to man more appreciated by him, it is a spiritual value. To the convinced and utterly thorough Epicurean even the greatest painting would remain a sensate value, because, no matter how sublime the aesthetic appeal, it would remain only an appeal to the senses and an enjoyment sought for its own sake. Likewise, to the lowest drunkard the sacrificial wine would represent only a sensate value as long as he had no sense whatsoever of the rôle it might play in the re-enactment of the sacrifice of Calvary. True, it is probably dangerous for the pure sensatist to toy with such values, if he is to remain a sensatist. For he is treading the very ground of miracles. The

15

great book, the painting, the music is pregnant with possibilities of spiritual appeal and many is the erstwhile convinced Epicurean who approached the Muses' gifts only
for the delectation of his senses and soon found the spark
of the divine, always latent in such gifts, kindling the fires
of his own soul. Or the drunkard ignorantly touching the
sacrificial wine may touch so close to Godhead as to be
forced out of his pure materialism, even if the "miracle"
should take no stranger form than a priest's prohibiting
the potential sacrilege. It is certain that to deal with the
highest sensate values is always to court the spiritual. But
conceivably they can remain only sensate.

Thus, at any level, high, middle, or low, sensate values
are rooted in the philosophy which holds to the primacy
of life, which looks upon life as an end in itself without
much concern for other ulterior ends, and which, therefore, holds that life should be openly and manifestly
passed as agreeably and pleasantly and comfortably and
richly as possible. Hellenistic Greece, Rome, the post-thir-
teenth century worlds have expended their energies, devoted their time to gaining things, objects, pleasant sensations and situations, multiplying them, increasing them,
holding on to them, protecting them, rendering them accessible to the greatest number for their happiness, enjoyment, and comfort. The western world for the past
five centuries—as the Hellenistic and Roman worlds a
thousand years before—has been concerned principally
with that which flattered its senses and appealed to them
in pleasing, interesting, or challenging ways.

The sensate worlds are accordingly worlds which delight in pleasure and comfort, in production and commerce
and industry, in wealth, both that which is stored and that
which is creatively active. They put their faith or their

admiration in the tangible things of earth: in machines, in roads, in dams, in aqueducts, in buildings, and colosseums and sky-scrapers, in fleets and armies, in comfort and wealth and power, in the manifest proofs of visible greatness. They cultivate production and science, particularly applied science, since these multiply for the sensate peoples their sources of comfort and pleasure and enjoyment.

The more daring and active members of sensate societies are adventurers and planners and builders. They open up new areas which the imagination of their more ordinary fellows could scarcely envision. In undertakings of discovery and conquest they throw open vast stretches of geographical space for the use and enjoyment of their contemporaries and those who come after them. Or they establish monumental businesses which afford opportunities for work and earning money, for getting, having, and enjoying upon the part of millions, opportunities which in their manifold ramifications surpass the sensate potentialities of new geographical spaces. The mildly daring and active members of sensate societies do similar things on a much smaller scale: They deal in regions, not in nations and continents. They are the successful business people, manufacturers, merchants, and inventors. Most members of a sensate society are, however, not adventuresome or daring. Their primary interest is in sensate comfort and in sensate happiness. They cultivate and cherish comfortable homes and cities; they seek gadgets and pleasant situations; they throng shows and games and spectacles. In all these areas they are absorbers more often than they are creators of sensate benefits: or else they help to spread what their more daring fellows have planned. They are devoted to things and to sensations. They want to sense, chiefly to enjoy. Their getting and having are usually only

17

means to the most dominant sensate goal, the enjoying. It is only the more daring and adventuresome sensate spirits whose getting and having and enjoying are so sweeping in their scope that they also make possible the getting and having and enjoying on the part of countless other millions of less bold spirits. The members of a sensate society are principally interested in what is to them the "reality" and power and success of the everyday world. Those who can accumulate the largest amount of tangible evidence of these criteria of value or who are most active in promoting or creating them are the successful and honored men of a sensate society.

The sensate "heroes" are statesmen, scientists, explorers, discoverers, inventors, lawgivers, and military leaders, *successful* writers, artists, and musicians, and orators, Solon, Pliny, Cicero, Newton, Bach, Hannibal, Caesar, Euclid, Lincoln, Rembrandt, *etc.;* and at a lower level closer to the decline of the sensate culture, the pamphleteers, politicians, engineers, bankers, magnates and captains of industry, builders of bridges and aqueducts, machines and dams, and the satirists, Archimedes, Pompey, Rousseau, Voltaire, Aristophanes, Marx, Martial, Juvenal, Ford, Robespierre, Edison, *etc.;* and in the full decadence of the sensate culture the sensate "heroes" become the tinselled and "glamor" show-offs, the economic prestidigitators and barkers, the epigonic technicians who substitute technique for genuine creativity, the muscle-boys, charioteers, gladiators, bull-fighters, football and baseball players, band leaders; and genuine agitators, the rebels and revolutionary leaders; and finally the sub-stratum types, gangsters, prostitutes, criminals, all these decadent types devoid of a real creativity of a higher sensate order; their main role seems to be a negative one of disgusting fairly decent people with the dying order without giving them a positive incentive to create a new one.

Nature of the dawning world of the spirit

The other type of test of value at various times dominant in the West and struggling into emergence in our present Renaissance to be again supreme is a spiritual test of value. In a spiritual culture the prime tests of value are rooted in the supra- and ultra- mundane, in the uplift of the human spirit into the highest realms to which it is capable of attaining. The spiritual cultures of the West, the world of the Hebrew prophets, of Homer and Hesiod and Aeschylos and Sophocles, and of the Middle Ages, have put their tests of value in God, in the soul, the *psyché*, the *anima*, in heaven, in sanctity, in absolute truth and absolute standards of morality. They have stressed the primacy of the things of God, not those of men, the primacy of things unseen, not those seen. Paul expresses it very succinctly: "We look not at the things which are seen, but at the things which are not seen. For the things which are seen are temporal; but the things which are not seen are eternal. If any man among you seem to be wise in the world, let him become a fool, that he may be wise. For the wisdom of this world is foolishness with God. . . . Let no man, therefore, glory in men."[1] St. John, the Apostle, equally succinctly expresses the rejection by those who live in the spirit of the primacy of sensate values:

"Love not the world nor the things which are in the world. If any man love the world. the charity of the Father is not in him. For all that is in the world is the concupiscence of the flesh and the concupiscence of the eyes, and the pride of life, which is not of the Father."[2]

Spiritual cultures consider themselves in the hands of

19

God, trust in Him, see in Him the source of their every thought, seek reconciliation and harmony with Him. Thus, at every act and thought of the Homeric heroes a god is at hand prompting them, even in their most elementary and automatic acts. Homeric men are in the hands of the gods, who have ulterior purposes for them, even in the automatic acts of self-defense and self-preservation. Nausica of the Phaecians goes a-washing because of the promptings of Athene, who makes the mortal girl assist in carrying out the divine will with regard to the hero.[3] Ino Leucothea and Athene help the exhausted Odysseus as he swims to the island of the Phaecians in the most elementary acts of self-preservation, prompting him now to cling to a log, now grasp a rock, now spit out the imbibed seawater, now to seek shelter from the breakers.[4] The whole universe is in the hands of God and seeks harmony with Him. Goddess Calypso herself must yield her beloved Odysseus because Zeus has willed it. "It is in no wise possible to make void the purpose of Zeus".[5] Aged Phoinix explains to Achiles about the reconciliatory power of prayer.

> "Gods' hearts by incense and reverent vows and drink offering and burnt offering men turn with prayer so oft as anyone transgresses and commits sins. . . . Prayers of penitence are daughters of great Zeus . . . that have their task to go in the steps of sin. . . . Sin goes before them and makes men fall but prayer follows behind to heal the harm."[6]

Similar is the mood of the omnipotence of God over the littleness of man in *Job*.

The spiritual cultures of the West have either ignored everyday, earth-earthy reality, been rather indifferent to it, or definitely refused to make it a prime criterion of truth, just as Hellenistic Greece, megalopolitan Rome, and the modern world have largely ignored eternity or heaven, or, at least, relegated them to a not too obtrusive place well symbolized in our time by the movie or song, "Heaven Can Wait."

The heroes of a spiritual culture are God, the Divine Family, the Virgin, the Saints, prophets like Moses and Jeremiah, martyrs, holy men, women, and children, and, if the culture is a pagan and polytheistic one, a whole series of gods, demi-gods, children of gods, vestal virgins, nature spirits, fairies, all the folk of the "unseen" world. If a spiritual culture chooses its heroes from the everyday world, its concept of the heroic in them is quite different from that of a sensate, utilitarian society. It divinizes the everyday, respects sanctity and virginity, austerity, even asceticism; where the sensate divests man of his nobility and dignity, ranking him with the "other" mammals, a higher primate, a spiritual civilization puts a halo around him and either figuratively or literally calls him a son of God and heir to the Kingdom of Heaven.

The nature of our time, thus, is that of a Renaissance of a spiritual world. The old world in which man has prized the things of this earth above all else is fast slipping from his grasp. It had to, for our world for the past six or seven hundred years has been a wrong world. When Christ says, "Lay not up for yourselves treasures on earth which moth and rust corrupt and thieves break through and steal, but rather lay up for yourselves treasures in Heaven where moth and rust corrupt not nor thieves break through and steal", or when He says, "What doth it profit a man if he gain the whole world and lose his immortal soul?", He is emphasizing both what is wrong with a world like our own and the Roman, and what we should do about it. That is, any civilization which puts its first tests of value in power and wealth and armies, in machines and dams and buildings, in pleasures of eye and touch and taste, will literally explode.

Modern man has two alternatives. First, either he must see that the world of might and power and armies, of materialism, is not a right world and must change of his own free will into a society which treasures most the values of the Kingdom of God. Or, secondly, if he refuses to realize the wrongness of his materialistic standards, then those things which he prizes will be torn from him by force of physical necessity, by war and revolution, by repeated calamity, until modern man, stripped of his material treasures, will be forced to find God the hard way, because all that will be left will be God. That is, modern man either of his own free will choice or by force of necessity will come to learn the truth of Christ: "My kingdom is not of this world."

To realize the nature of our age is the most important secular act of our time. For we must be forces either of action or reaction. To the degree that we ally ourselves with the forces for God we are creative. To the degree that we ally ourselves with the forces against Him we are reactionary. Our time can move into its future only as rapidly as men move with it. Those who cling to the values of this world as foremost values are the blind forces of reaction in our day. They are not only the Communists and other totalitarians who by their extreme materialism are among the worst reactionaries of our time. But reactionaries are equally all those members of any group, any party, any country, who put the things of this world before the things of God. Such men, be they sincere or not, be they honest, or be they only greedy in clinging to the things of this world before all else, delay the free will choice of modern man to come back to his God. If they delay it too long, they leave only the second alternative to modern man, namely, to be stripped completely, so that he may seek his God. For no matter how much the Communists or the materialists of any sort may shout against it, the true nature of our time is a transition into the world of the future when the underlying philosophy of living will be the emphasis of Christ!

The threat of our time

It must not be imagined for a moment that a spiritual culture is a primitive culture or inferior to a sensate culture as many of our contemporaries might quickly assume. The earliest traces of Western man indicate, in fact, that the sensate culture is the more primitive of the two. The earliest Western culture, about which we have satisfyingly adequate knowledge, the Creto-Mycenean culture, was very obviously sensate. It was followed by the highly developed spiritual culture of early Greece, whose fine atmosphere we can still, as it were, figuratively breathe through the medium of some of the greatest works of Western literature, those of Homer and Hesiod and Aeschylos and Sophocles and Plato. But also in the generally nebulous areas of "pre-history" it is clear that the sensate cultures are more primitive than the spiritual ones.

Paleolithic man of the First Stone Age was very demonstrably sensate in the few remains which he has left of himself, mainly in his sensate art cut in the caves of Western Europe and Southern Africa. It is exclusively a reproduction of empirical objects and scenes of his everyday life in which he was chiefly interested or occupied, animals, hunting, fishing, eating, and the like.

On the other hand, the Neolithic culture of the Late Stone Age, a much more highly developed culture, was just as obviously a spiritual culture with little or no interest in empirical reality but with its gaze fixed heavenward. Thus, from the very dawn of history it has been a more developed spiritual culture in the West which has followed an older sensate one. If there is any accusation of primitiveness which can be laid against either of the two types of culture, it cannot be laid against our spiritual cultures.

It must be equally stressed that a spiritual culture is not an inferior one. In fact, unless the transition period away from the preceding sensate culture is so blindly chaotic and physically ruinous that it seriously mars the dawning spiritual culture, the spiritual culture seems guaranteed to be the superior one. It has a higher truth and a more adequate criterion of values than those of the poor obfuscated senses and beplagued passions of man. Pre-Hellenistic Greek culture was far superior either to the Creto-Mycenean culture which preceded it or the Hellenistic and megalopolitan Roman civilizations which followed it. Its literature, its art, its architecture, its ideas, its philosophy, its moral and epistemological standards were far superior to those of its sensate predecessor or successor. It had far more adequate truth. Spiritual cultures like those represented by the Hebrew prophets or by the greatest spiritual culture of all, the Christian medieval period, had more adequate truth still—the truth of divine Revelation. What may to us seem to have marred the Christian medieval world was really nothing inherent in the culture itself. What may seem to have marred it was the fact that the West was so physically shaken by the protracted decadence and prolonged death agony of sensate Rome that much of the medieval world, superficially at least, appears needlessly scarred by the aftermaths of the Roman débâcle, needlessly, that is, if sensate man of the Imperium Romanum had not been so blind that his world *had* to be shaken to its very foundations before he would relinquish his grasp on his lifeless, materialistic, pagan values. The plagues, the wars, the upheavals and migrations, the invasions, the impoverishment which marred so much of European life at various times during the Middle Ages were not inherent in any teaching of Christ by which the medieval world lived. They were traceable, directly or indirectly, to the fact that so many areas of thought and knowledge of Imperial Rome, which were not necessarily bad in themselves and which frequently were even good and which could have been very beneficial if they could have survived and been incorporated in the medieval, Christian culture, were lost in the terrific chaos of dissolution which was required to shake and force and pry and shock and tear the Roman decadents loose from their over-ripe, and frequently foul and festering, sensate tests of value.

This is also precisely the threat which impends now over the arising spiritual culture, the new Christian Renaissance of our time. *Per se* it is almost guaranteed to be a better culture than the modern sensate one. But the physical jarrings which modern sensate man may by his own stupidity and blindness insist on inflicting on himself may be so terrible and so shattering, on a scale unprecedented in the West, of which the dissolution of Rome may be but the palest foreshadowing, that the arising spiritual culture, like the medieval one, may be marred and scarred and impoverished beyond all need, simply because of the folly and blindness and wilful complacency of our time. So much of the sensate world, its objects, its treasures, the great knowledge and products of science, which could be very helpful in the dawning spiritual civilization, will unfortunately doubtless be dissolved into thin air if the obfuscation of modern sensate man persists.

Past spiritual cultures

The medieval Christian period has without question been the most thoroughly spiritual civilization of Western man to date. The world of Homer and Hesiod and Aeschylos and the world of the Hebrew prophets are like it, however, in spirit, differing only in degree and secondary externals.

The Homeric heroes are not a-work primarily in terms of the values of the everyday world about them. They are *sub specie aeternitatis,* under the dome of divinity and eternity. The purposes and plans and will of the gods have set their mark upon them, and they are instruments of a divine purpose whose goals they only dimly comprehend. They consider themselves in the hands of the gods, whose work they do. A power from beyond, greater than that of everyday empirical reality, impends over them, gives them their criteria over life's values, makes them heroic.

Thus, too, it is with the heroes of the great Greek tragedians. Let us consider, for example, Sophocles' *Oedipus.* By the standards of everyday reality, his parents and Oedipus himself do everything reasonable to avoid the divine oracle which hangs over him even before he is born. The workings of the divine intellect, inscrutable to the mere reason of man, have, however, decreed that this babe in the womb shall when grown to manhood be the murderer of his father and the incestuous lover of his mother. Horror driven, the parents, each in his own way, try to prevent this prophecy of bestial foulness and ineffable evil. The father seeks the destruction of the babe, and the mother, following a middle course, speeds it out of the country, so that she may never see it or hear from

it again. Oedipus, reared in a neighboring country by
foster parents whom he believed to be his own, learning
of the dreadful oracle which hangs over him, flees with
all speed the land and mother and father he believes to
be his own in order to put as much distance as possible
between himself and the fulfillment of such frightfulness.
But, instead, he comes into his true native land, by acci-
dent kills his father, in innocence marries his mother, and
fastens the last link in the dire catena of fate. The will
and purpose and criteria of the gods thus are made manifest over the will and purpose and criteria of man. The
dominant criteria of reality are not what man wills and
foresees and does but what a god wills and foresees and
brings to pass. The direct prophetical revelation of divinity
is greater than any earthly empirical sensate reality. What
seems "real" to Oedipus and his parents proves foolish
in terms of the greater wisdom of the gods.

It should be observed that in some respects, at least,
the Greek spiritual and moral code was an even stricter
one than that of the medieval Christian world. The Greek
code holds that parricide and incest in and by themselves
are horrible and gravely punishable acts even when their
committers do them unknowingly. According to Christian
philosophy on the other hand man sins only to the degree
that he knows he sins. As long as Oedipus and his parents
did everything in their power to avoid the sin foretold to
them, they are not sinners according to Christian philosophy. Yet, the cleavage between the Greek spiritual and
moral codes and Christian ones is more superficial than
real. For there comes a time when Oedipus and his mother
sin knowingly. And it is at this point that the Greek retribution of divine anger and Christian condemnation coin-
cide. The first time when Oedipus really sins according to

our Christian concept is after the shocking acts of parricide and incest have been accomplished. In spite of the ever increasing proof of their dreadful state he and his mother prefer to be blind, refuse to admit the evidence which incontrovertibly is rendering Oedipus culpable of parricide and him and his mother guilty of incest and foulness. They are driven into the vengeance of fate because they have preferred for at least a few short hours to abide by that which is foul and nasty, which is against the solemn law of decency. The prime tests of value holding sway in their world are not in the passions and whim of man but in the absolute unchanging law of God. He who sins against this law, this absolute, unchanging commandment, is guilty unto death, no matter the manner of his sinning. The tests of value of the supra-mundane in the *Oedipus* world are supreme. It is, however, only superficially that the Greek moral code seems to be more rigid and austere than the Christian one. Retribution in the Greek drama is justified easily by Christian philosophy, because it is only from the time that Oedipus and his mother sin knowingly that they *are* punished by the Greek criterion of justice, or are punishable by the Christian one. It is from the moment of their realized guilt that *Oedipus* could be just as completely a Christian play as a Greek one; and this is really the period of concentration of Sophocles' play, which, like all classical drama, is psychological, taking place in the *psyché,* the soul, not in the areas of action and superficial agitation like so many modern plays. The two moral codes, the Greek and the Christian, essentially fuse, we see, to become one. It is a most interesting phenomenon in the history of the two greatest spiritual civilizations of our West, those of Greece and the medieval world, that their criteria of truth, their

28

hierarchies of value are so close to one another. The fact that Greek philosophy and Greek literature were so widely known in the Mediterranean world made the spread of the Christian spiritual civilization so much easier than it might otherwise have been. The Christian spiritual Renaissance of the first centuries A. D. received much support from the Greek spiritual civilization, which, even if it had been pushed into the background by the sensate world of Rome, still possessed some remnants of life in the literature and philosophy which had in some form or other survived from old Greece. Likewise, all through the Christian culture of the medieval period the philosophy and criteria of truth and hierarchies of value of ancient Greece were fused into and incorporated with those of the Christian world, from Paul and Tertullian and St. Augustine to Albertus Magnus and St. Thomas D'Aquino. In fact, it may be truly stated that pure Christianity sank its roots most ineradicably in Mediterranean lands such as Italy and France and Spain, where the soil had been prepared for it by some contact with the literature and philosophy of ancient Greece which seeped into these lands not only from Greece itself but also from the cultural and intellectual life of Rome which had so little understanding for the Greek thought it was passing on. Whereas in the pagan Germanic North, where the spiritual civilization of Greece was little borne, Christianity never succeeded ordinarily in striking such deep root; and there it fell apart more rapidly, and there was dissolved more thoroughly the Christian unity of medieval spiritual Europe in the terrible storms of the new arising sensate paganism which swept over the world after the thirteenth century. Greece and the medieval world, no matter how much they differed in externals, were sister spiritual worlds with sister tests of value, just as Rome and the modern world in spite of undeniable external differences are sisters by their common sensate, utilitarian, materialistic, pragmatic, pagan tests of value.

Quite similar to the hierarchy of values of Greece and medieval Christianity are the spiritual tests of value from the world of the Hebrew prophets. Man proposes, but God disposes. The criteria of the everyday empirical world yield before the tests of value of the eternal.

> "So spake the Lord to Job: 'Who is this that wrappeth up sentences in unskillful words? . . . . Where wast thou when I laid the foundations of the earth? . . . . Didst thou since thy birth command the morning and show the dawning of the day its place? who had put wisdom into the heart of man?' "7

> "The lofty eyes of man are humbled and the haughtiness of men shall be made to stoop: and the Lord alone shall be exalted."8

What true wisdom man is considered to have is believed by the prophets to be the direct gift of God. Man lies in the hand of God. The real truth is viewed to be not that of the senses but that which God reveals directly to man in His Commandments and through His prophets.

Our nearest spiritual culture, the medieval world

The spiritual civilization to which we stand closest in point of time, however, is that of the Middle Ages. Our future spiritual civilization into which we are moving obviously will and can be no restoraton of the Middle Ages, in fact will differ very much in countless important externals from them. It will be an entirely new civilization. It will not take up where the Middle Ages left off any more than modernity, in spite of similar tests of value to Rome, was able to begin with the forms and setting of the world prevailing at the time the Roman world exploded. Its forms and methods will be neither a restoration nor a continuation of the Middle Ages. It will rather be a civilization setting out on entirely new and undared pathways, challenging the best efforts of man. Yet, at the same time, in spite of its newness, the dawning civilization will be closer to the medieval world in its spirit and tests of value than it will to any other world which we have known in the past, closer to the Middle Ages than it will be to the world of the Hebrew prophets or that of ancient Greece.

Between us and the world of the Hebrew prophets and of ancient Greece stand the most important spiritual events which have happened in all Western history, the birth, the ministry, the establishment of the *ecclesia,* the Passion, the Crucifixion, and Resurrection of Christ. Christ was the real founder of the most recent spiritual society, the one which overthrew the decadent sensate world of Rome and which was developed by the Apostles and disciples and Fathers and philosophers of the Church and brought to fruition by the millions of men and women who constituted the medieval Christian society. Our most recent spiritual culture lived by the hierarchy of values established by Christ. The life, the suffering, the teachings of Christ gave the dominant tests of value by which men were to live for the first thousand years after the dissolution of sensate Rome. The forces which were to make this one thousand year future were already strongly at work in the Roman world of the first century A. D. The Apostles and disciples of Christ by the written and spoken word had sown the seed for the future. The New Testament had been written. Christianity was spreading throughout the Mediterranean world. Medieval Christian civilization had in a very real sense begun in the first century A. D.

From then on the future was destined to be a Christianity of a high spiritual order which was to become the dominant religion of the Western world. More significantly still in terms of our future, Christianity survived, at least among certain groups, the great change in tests of value brought in by the last Renaissance. The rebirth of the old Roman materialistic and pagan tests of value of the senses in the last Renaissance admittedly affected Christianity, introduced some elements which are still in conflict within the body of Christendom. It, in fact, corrupted certain areas of Christianity to a sufficient degree to enable them to exist more readily in a world which lived chiefly by the senses in contradiction to the basic emphasis of genuine Christianity. That is, the modern sensate post-Renaissance world has had as its members not only the pagans and the materialists, who harmonized perfectly with modern tests of value, but also part Christians: one-tenth-Christians, one-third-Christians, one-half-Christians, who performed rather astounding and interesting somersaults in order to hold on to certain areas of Christianity and at the same time live quite sincerely according to the pragmatic, materialistic sensate tests of value. And, obviously, also there have been Christians in the modern post-Renaissance world. Christianity, no matter how modified and divided, has survived and served as enough spiritual restraint in our modern world as frequently to prevent its becoming so completely and paganly sensate as was the world of Rome. Christianity is also surviving the travail of the contemporary transition of our time from one test of value upon the part of the West to another. It will emerge certainly much stronger and purer than it has been in centuries. The West has definitely and permanently chosen Christianity as its chief religion. If the West is to have religion at all, that religion will be predominantly Christianity. It is here to stay, "and the gates of Hell shall not prevail against it." Therefore, if we are entering again into a society whose chief tests of value will be spiritual ones, we shall have a world of Christian spiritual values.

It is in the Middle Ages that we shall find a world closest akin to our new world of the spirit. The new world will certainly differ very much from the Middle Ages in a multitude of externals. But our future will be close to the Middle Ages in spirit. Christ and His teachings will be the foundation stones of the next world of the spirit just as much as they were those of the last. It is this fact which inescapably will render our coming society of the spirit closer to the medieval world than it will be to that of ancient Greece or that of the Hebrew prophets. Our attention will, therefore, in this work be much more frequently centered on the tests of value of the Middle Ages than on Hebrew or Greek spiritual cultures, as we examine the nature of our New Renaissance of the Spirit. We shall be quoting much more frequently from Christ than from Homer or Aeschylos or Plato or Aristotle or Job or Jeremiah. Jesus rather than they will be the main source of our tests of value of the future. Christ will dominate the new world.

Outlines of the future

The outlines of the new world under Christ are already taking shape. National barriers must be broken down. As in the Middle Ages the citizen of the new world must first be a child of God before he is a Frenchman,

33

a Pole, a Greek, an Englishman. At the outset of our now passing modern world new altars of nationalism so often replaced the altars of God over the face of Europe. The loyalties which the medievalist could pay to God have in the modern world often been usurped by the demands of national prejudices and hates and by materialistic, often greedy, nationalistic goals. These were, indeed, poor altars and hollow loyalties to replace those to an omnipotent God, all just, all loving, all good.

In our time we are seeing these new altars crumble in a crescendo of mounting horror. Men everywhere are learning to their sorrow that nations cannot pursue a course of individualistic anarchy at the expense of their fellow nations. They are learning that the competitions and greeds and rivalries and hates among nations will have to be curbed or else all civilization will be threatened. Either nations will learn that they must live under God or else they will pull down Samson-like the very pillars of their existence on their heads.

The false, pagan, nationalistic altars are demanding close to their last possible sacrifices, will soon cease— through either the blindness or wisdom of modern men. For we are witnessing that nations cannot trample rough-shod over the rights of other nations without bringing down upon themselves the anger of an avenging God implemented by the outraged and righteous indignation of men stung to a fury of resistance against evil. Nations can inherit the resistance of almost an entire world. The nations of our time cannot much longer continue their mad quest for power and wealth and survive the onslaught of modern war that their policies entail.

In overthrowing the altars of God in Western civilization and establishing those of national group, we post-

Renaissance modern men have re-established the law of the jungle. In our time we are literally close to a *bellum omnium contra omnes*. Nations refusing to abide by the law of God have each pursued their own advantages at the expense of their neighbors. Divorced from higher divine law, the rights and goals they have pursued have had to be pursued at the expense of the rights and goals of others. Might has replaced justice as a norm among nations, might and materialistic "self-interest".

Ironically, the altars of nationalism are now close to their final draining. Modern man faces two alternatives in his worship at these altars. Either they drain wealth and substance to the point of exhausting his sensate treasures as he prepares for war and engages in war. And the war itself in its ever increasing efficiency of ruin destroys his national treasures, his very home and sources of employment, renders national existence impossible. Or else man ceases voluntarily his *bellum omnium contra omnes* to live once more in harmony with his brothers under God. The long range result is the same. But the choice of alternatives is one between madness and self-destruction and ruin or wisdom and prudence and salvation.

The outlines of the future begin now to be delineated. Nations must live under God. They must be bound by a sense of duty and responsibility. They will know that their existence and rights cannot be purchased at the expense of the existence and rights of others, know that what affects one affects the other, even the least of them, know that the only equilibrium which maintains the equilibrium of all rests in the balances of God.

Nations must acquire a new simplicity and a new humility, either be forced into it by the hard and awful way of utter chaos and destruction or by their free will choice.

Literally, they must become as little children trusting to the Father instead of to their own futile and exhaustible might. A child is simple and without duplicity and useless complication. It is conscious of its weakness, its dependence on its parents, that it has need of receiving everything from the love and kindness of others. It is disposed to believe the truth it receives from those it loves, to place absolute trust and confidence in the giver of its gifts and to love the giver with all its childish, trusting heart. It follows that nations living under God, the Giver of all gifts, must manifest equal confidence and trust and humility and faith. The outlines of the future demand that nations and the men in them must show forth the virtues of belief in God, hope in Him, and Love of Him. Nations and men must perform the acts of Faith, Hope, and Charity—or perish with their populations from the earth.

The outlines of the future demand that the hungry on earth be fed not out of a spirit of superior bounty and "self-interest" but in the spirit of brotherly charity, for all men are children of God, brothers under God, having a right to share in the gifts of God, apportioned for all His children, even those, yea, especially those, who were our enemies, when we were moved by false ideals and false gods and false goals and worshipped at our false national altars.

Justice must come to dominate the relations between nations and the relations between groups and individuals within the nations - - justice and a sense of mutual duty, mutual responsibility, mutual obligation. A just government recognizes in its acts both within and without the nation that its power is limited by the basic human liberties and human rights of its members and its neighbors. In the new world a nation can exist only when it is ready for sacrifice in the interest of all, sacrifice motivated not merely by "self-interest" but principally by love of God and man. What is true of a single nation must be true of the family of nations which cannot escape the close proximity and interdependence which are inherent in the very physical structure of the modern world.

For the Incarnation of God into Man entailed as its long-range obligation the duty for man to work and devote his energies and his talent and his genius and his prayers for the establishment of the Kingdom of God. In taking upon Himself the sins of the world God has freed man from the otherwise irreparable and infinite results of the Divine Anger and challenges man to restore himself in the Redeeming Grace of God, challenges him to re-establish as much as possible his state before the Fall. The Incarnation does not imply that man can throw off all the results of his Fall from Paradise. But it does mean that God has done His part in removing the infinite effects of man's revolt against God. It means that man must take up the challenge to strive to do his part too, helped in every direction by God. The Incarnation was veritably the beginning of a process which cannot stop until the whole universe is redeemed, comes to know and serve and love its God, until the nations of the earth bow once more before Him. It is a universal Kingdom that God has vistaed for us, sacramental through and through because God and man should in any proper order be in-separably united in the Harmony of the Supreme Will, be brothers under God and partakers in His Divine Nature, be united in the Mystical Body of Christ.

To the pagan, modern materialistic world there is danger in even this idealism. It must not look at the great material goods which a proper order can attain as goals in themselves. We should work for the right order not principally because of the reward but principally because we love God Who loves righteousness and we should want to establish that which is pleasing to Him. It is perfectly true that if we love God and seek first His Kingdom and His Justice, all the material goods of the world will be added unto us in a bounty no civilization of the past has ever dreamed of. But in the abundance of the gift the new world must always love principally the Giver. The greatest of all the supernatural virtues is Charity, the supernatural Love of God for His own sake. The new world must be vibrantly alive with the Love of God.

This will mark a complete break with modern materialistic tests of value. The new world will be sister under the skin to the medieval world destroyed by the last Renaissance, a better world if we choose, yet a sister. Modernity loves and worships the gift. But this will be torn from it by force if that is the only way to enable modernity to find its way to the Giver. The Giver is the fount which thirsting mankind must find. How incomplete is the gift without knowledge and Love of the Giver! How mistaken and inadequate and wrong has been modernity with only its gift!

The material things, the terrestrial riches and gifts, are not wrong in themselves, but they are wrong when pursued as first values. They are also very dangerous. There is not one word of Christ's which warns of the dangers of poverty. Passage after passage of the New Testament, however, warns of the dangers of riches, how they ensnare and enmesh the soul. Our age, even if it is blind and has to be stripped of everything to get into the future, will not be dealt with cruelly from the All-Wisdom of God. Our age may need to be taught an awful lesson.

Perhaps the only way it can be taught is through utter dispossession. Our age has had so little insight into the blessing of poverty under God that it may have to get that insight terribly hard and terribly thoroughly before it is worthy to enjoy the gifts of God again.

Yet, this harshness of teaching is not necessary, nor is it God's demand. It depends on man. God made His great gifts for man's good. They can be used for that when they do not blind man's vision against the Giver. Poverty and ugliness and despoilment and chaos riding over the face of the earth are not in God's necessary plan unless man brings them on himself. But man needs to be brought back into the graces and wisdom of the spiritual Middle Ages and gain again a proper perspective of truth and reality and God.

A society governed by spiritual tests of value cannot make the material gifts of God of prime importance: "My Kingdom is not of this world." When Christ exclaims, "What doth it profit a man even if he gain the whole world and lose his immortal soul?", He is laying down the prime test of value of a spiritual civilization as opposed to a sensate one. He holds *all* the values of the sensate, empirical world to be as nothing in comparison with the salvation of the immortal soul. The real thing to Him is not all machines and power and wealth and armies and victories and commerce and industry but eternity and the lot of the human soul in it. "Lay not up for yourselves treasures on earth where thieves break through and steal and moth and rust corrupt but lay up for yourselves treasures in Heaven." Here again He is stressing that the prime tests of value are not in the here and now but with Him in the eternal. The everyday is to take care of itself without first thought being given to it. The Father

39

knows the needs it may bring. Man is not to worry principally about them.

The essence of medieval Christian civilization

The medieval world in giving first place to spiritual tests of value and following literally the teachings of Christ placed its principal tests of value in God, not in the *things* of this earth, but in the *reality* of eternity. The temporary life on earth was of secondary importance, a mere testing ground for the more enduring life to come. The main concerns of the medieval Christian culture were with the most efficacious manners of loving and serving God in the temporary proving period so as to be happy with Him in eternity. Its tests of value were not centered in earth but in Heaven or Hell, the glories and joys of eternity, or its sufferings and torments imposed by Justice. Sometimes it ignored everyday reality, despised, avoided it; more frequently it accepted it as an unavoidable, even ineluctable evil. It was part of the Cross which man, like his Savior, had to bear. It lived literally recognizing the validity of the teachings and emphases of Jesus and the New Testament as ideal norms.

"I say to you, be not solicitous for your life, what you shall eat, nor for your body, what you shall put on. . . . Be not solicitous, therefore, saying, 'What shall we eat,' or 'What shall we drink,' or wherewith shall we be clothed?' For after all these things do the pagans seek. . . . Seek ye first the Kingdom of God and His justice."9

"For we brought nothing into this world and certainly we can carry nothing out. But having food and wherewith to be covered with these we are content. For they that will become rich fall into temptation and into the snare of the devil and into many unprofitable and hurtful desires, which drown men into destruction and perdition. For the desire of money is the root of all evils; which some

coveting have erred from the faith, and have entangled themselves
into many sorrows. But thou, O man of God, fly these things; and
pursue justice, godliness, faith, charity, patience, mildness. Fight
the good fight of faith, lay hold on eternal life, whereunto thou
art called."10

"If any man among you seem to be wise in this world, let him become a fool, that he may be wise. For the wisdom of this world is
foolishess with God. . . . Let no man, therefore, glory in men."11

"If the world hate you, know that it hated me before you. If you
had been of the world, the world would love its own; but because
you are not of the world, but I have chosen you out of the world,
therefore, the world hateth you. . . . If they have persecuted me,
they will also persecute you."12

"We look not at the things which are seen, but at the things which
are not seen. For the things which are seen are temporal. But the
things which are not seen are eternal."13

"What shall it profit, my brethren, if a man say he hath faith but
not works? Shall faith be able to save him? And if a brother or a
sister be naked and want daily food and one of you say to them:
'Go in peace; be ye warmed and filled,' yet give them nothing of
those things which are necessary for the body, what shall it profit?
So faith also if it hath not works is dead in itself."14

"I say to you, walk in the spirit and you shall not fulfill the lusts
of the flesh. For the flesh lusteth against the spirit and the spirit
against the flesh, for they are contrary one to the other. Now the
works of the flesh are . . . fornication, uncleanliness, immodesty,
luxury, idolatry, witchcrafts, enmities, contentions, emulations,
wraths, quarrels, dissensions, sects, envies, murders, drunken-
ness, reveling, and such like. . . . They who do such things shall not
obtain the Kingdom of God. But the fruit of the Spirit is charity,
joy, peace, patience, benignity, goodness, longanimity, mildness,
faith, chastity. . . . They that are Christ's have crucified the flesh
with its vices and concupiscenses."15

"And this is the judgment because the light of the world is come
into the world and men loved darkness rather than the light, for
their works were evil. For everyone that doth evil hateth the light,
and cometh not to the light, that his works may not be reproved,"16

"The world . . . hateth me because I give testimony that its works
are evil."17

41

With the usual many expected lapses from such demanding tests of value, the members of the medieval world tried to live to the best of their ability in accordance with such principles of Christ as laid down in the New Testament. This is not to say that all who tried to live by these precepts succeeded in abiding by them even quasi perfectly. Human frailty, man's penchant for evil, the weakened will which he inherited directly from his fall from Paradise, frequently rendered his keeping of such principles far from perfect. But medieval man tried to keep them. Even if he did not always keep them, in contrast to modern man he, at least, knew that they were absolute principles by which he *should* live.

A spiritual society will necessarily take such precepts most seriously. Medieval society certainly did so. It was an austere, Christian, disciplined society. Life on earth was but a preparation for the real eternal life to come. Life here below was not necessarily supposed to be pleasant or easy. Christ had made the Cross the symbol for man, and had made plain that he who followed Him would know hate and persecution and travail and suffering. Each man was to have his Cross. Life was a vale of tears. Christ had suffered, been deserted by all men, even by the faithful twelve who usually followed Him, was crucified, died apparently an utter failure, crying out to His Father in Heaven, "Why hast thou abandoned me?". Surely, suffering and travail were to be expected by those who followed in the footsteps of such a leader.

The emphasis of the medieval world was, therefore, away from everyday material reality. Its tests of value were not rooted in the here and now but in the eternal. No age has been less devoted to the matters of earth than was the medieval period at its height. Its very soul was Christian. Its books—except for the comparatively small corpus of pagan tinged material like the *fabliaux, Volksdichtung,* and the *Carmina Burana types*—were religious in nature, frequently comments, rephrasings, refurbishings of the New Testament. Its poems were hymns developed from New Testament themes. Its architecture was the New Testament frozen in stone, its paintings, its church windows the New Testament in color. In spite of the fact that Bibles were so hard to make and so few and precious that they had to be chained in the churches so as to be accessible to all, the New Testament was the very ambient in which the medievalist walked and breathed.

The business and commerce and money making in which Rome had gloried were no longer held to be the most admirable pursuits of men. The ancient Roman cities, the arenas, and aqueducts, and bridges fell into decay. Christians were loathe to lend money and sometimes even to engage in commerce. It was not infrequently considered wrong to sell an article for more than one had paid for it. Only non-Christians, like the Jews, might engage with untroubled consciences in commerce, although not rare Christian merchants seem not to have been over-burdened with *mea-culpas.* A thorough medievalist, like some of the Franciscans, if he had seen such an anachronism from our sensate world as a $100 gold piece, would have ground it into the earth with his foot so as to hide this source of sin from the eye of man. For riches and money were a source of temptation. The less one had of them, the better. Christ Himself had said: "How with difficulty shall they who have riches enter into the kingdom of God: it is easier for a camel to enter through the eye of a needle than it is for a rich man to enter into the Kingdom of God."

Hundreds of thousands of men and women, following the advice of Christ and the teachings of St. Paul, that virginity is a state preferable to marriage, entered the convents and cloisters and monasteries to spend their lives in fasting and prayer, in self-mortification and penance, in adoration of God, in studying and copying His divine Revelation to man. There are numerous examples of kings and queens, princes and princesses, who gave away all that they had, kingdoms, and power, and riches, to become humble workers in the vineyard of the Lord. The medievalists knew, as any spiritual society must know, that one cannot hold the gifts of earth to be prime values. They knew, as Christ knew, as anyone who lives by spiritual values *must* know, that the gifts of God should not blind the vision of man so as to hide the Giver.

"Be not solicitous about tomorrow for tomorrow will be solicitous about itself."[18]

"For everyone that asketh receiveth; and he that seeketh findeth; and to him that knocketh, it shall be opened."[19]

"Are not two sparrows sold for a farthing? And not one of them shall fall to the ground without your Father. . . . But the very hairs of your head are numbered."[20]

"Consider the lilies of the field, how they grow; they labor not, neither do they spin. But I say to you that not even Solomon in all his glory was arrayed as one of these. Now if God clothe in this manner the grass that is today in the field and tomorrow is cast into the oven, how much more you, O ye of little faith. . . . Your Father knoweth that you have need of these things. But seek ye first the Kingdom of God and His justice and all these things shall be added unto you."[21]

A spiritual culture accepts such ideas literally and putting first things first looks to the heavenly Father for its temporal sustenance. A sensate or materialistic society either shrugs its shoulders and calls such a philosophy impossible or trusts that by appearing to do, or making pretence to do, the "first things" of a spiritual society, it will be assured of getting its plentiful supply of the other things added to it. If the sensate society does not secure them, it will cease to pay even lip service, may become embittered and resentful, and may even throw out its God entirely, for the more obvious and manifest satisfactions of the moment. To a sensate civilization the maxim, "God helps them who help themselves", may mean anything from downright stealing to the materialistic effort of the poor boy who becomes wealthy and powerful by honesty, alert dealing, industry, and shrewdness; and in the latter case getting its God and its honors and its wealth all mixed up or fused into one, it will name a church or a college building after him and in hope of touching his "generosity" will award him an honorary doctorate at commencement time. In the best Yankee tradition such a sensate society will attend to its homilies and its Bible on Sundays so that its ledger may be prosperous on week days. It will willingly trade one day to the Lord, provided He do handsomely by it the other six, and will consider it a good bargain, indeed, to have "all these things", or, at least, a nice comfortable amount of them, added to it.

On the other hand, to a spiritual society the values of eternity are so dominantly first that all others recede before them. God chastises those whom He loves, does not make them prosperous. He visits them with trial and tribulation so that life is a valley of tears. The members of a spiritual society have no first care for earthly things. Their realities are not in the everyday world but in eternity. Its minimal earthly needs a spiritual society accepts literally and trustingly will be added in sufficient amount to sustain life and further the service of God. The great reality is not here and now. It is eternity. The earth-earthy is, at best, a testing course, a preparation for the dominant and permanent values of the life to come. The two types of Western culture, therefore, the sensate and the spiritual, resting on different tests of value interpret the world about them and man's purpose in it in quite different ways.

Irreconciliability of the two cultures

This difference in interpretation implies that what is real and true to one civilization, the sensate, can be unreal and false to the spiritual, and *vice versa*. St. Paul has stated this contradiction with a simplicity which is unequaled: "The wisdom *of this world* is foolishness *with God*." Unless one understands the two types of worlds contrasted by Paul, the sentence is a paradox. Without the all important phrase modifiers, the statement bluntly says that wisdom is foolishness. What Paul has admirably done here is to show the difference in the two types of tests of value. What is wise in a sensate civilization can be foolish in a spiritual one. What is real in a spiritual civilization may be unreal, even non-existent to a sensate society.

Of course, in a given type of civilization not all people are entirely sensate or entirely spiritual. But there is an unmistakable overtone of sensatism or spirituality at a given time. The majority of the members of a society recognize the validity of the dominant tests of values. They live by them, their whole civilization is based on them. In a sensate world the non-sensatists, non-materialists, non-utilitarians, non-pagans, are vaguely tolerated, scorned, ridiculed, mistreated, exiled, imprisoned, or done to death according to the degree of creativity or decadency of the period. In a spiritual society the sensatists and pagans are prayed for, pitied, shunned or envied according to the degree of creativity or decadency of the spiritual order. At all events, most people are sensatists or materialists in a world which places its hierarchy of values in things, sensations, power, armies, prestige, and wealth; most people are religious and spiritual in an age which places its tests of value in eternity. Or phrasing it another way, when the majority of people live by their senses, we have a sensate society; when the majority of people come to live by the spirit, we have a spiritual society. In both types of society some members, few or numerous, will lapse rather completely from the tests of value of the majority. At all times there are also some people who in varying degrees of sincerity, coupled with various mental somersaults, successfully or unsuccessfully try to fuse the two tests of value. But, in general, such tests of value are not fused by the culture as a whole and cannot be so fused. They are opposite cultures, mutually exclusive one of the other, mutually "dark ages" to one another. To each its opposite type is false and unreal, filled with darkness, evil, error, superstition, and a whole gamut of incomprehensibility.

This fact is the principal reason for the irreconciliability of the two types of civilization. The tests of value are so mutually exclusive one of the other that what is true to one is false to the other, what is wise to the one is foolish to the other. They look upon one another as periods of ignorance, darkness, lapses into error and superstition, regressions into a more primitive, lower, even semi-bestial order. Hence, they sincerely apply to one another the term of "dark ages". Every modern sensate schoolboy "knows" that the "Dark Ages" were a vague medieval period lying somewhere between the fall of Rome and the Protestant Revolt. They appear to him as a period of decay, ignorance, superstition, and disease. He has a quasi-vague, quasi-precise conception of them as ages when uncontrolled pestilences ravaged the cities and the countryside of Europe, when rapacious and lecherous priests domineered over a superstitious and unwashed rabble of ignorant humanity, held in unlettered serfdom by a cruel and designing feudal trio of lord and bishop and king, the lords spiritual and lords temporal. Ignorance, error, superstition, retrogression seem to him the earmarks of the age. Only many years of study and reading can remove from him his misconceptions and his miseducation concerning these ages, which are simply a different type of culture from his own. Few people, indeed, ever advance beyond an elementary misunderstanding of the great spiritual world which existed between the sensate world of Rome and the sensate world of today. It is a middle period, literally medieval, middle ages, between the sensate reality of the Roman yesterday and the sensate reality of the modern today.

If the modern sensatists are acquainted with the civilization and spirit of Rome, they understand it and recognize its kinship to their own world. But they are "lost" in the Middle Ages. Most of our modern sensatists are, of course, ignorant and scornful of any other time but their own. They really do not know Rome. They have no realization that their tests of value and standards and ideas would have been considered entirely modern and up-to-date in the Rome of Tiberius and Nero. But to all sensatists, lettered and unlettered, the spiritual world of 400 A. D. to 1200 is an uncomfortable, foreign period. The wiser sensatists are not entirely satisfied with the term

"Dark Ages", for they find always vaguely astir in them some of the undercurrents which were strongly reborn in the thirteenth to the fifteenth centuries to make their modern world of today. But even to the wiser sensatists it is a period of relative darkness, ignorance, superstition, pestilence, famine, crusades, fanaticism, and calamity. They cannot entirely rid themselves of the elementary misconceptions and miseducation of the sensate schoolboy.

Even these wiser sensatists are so immersed in their own tests of value that they cannot comprehend the greatness of a period so different from theirs as were the Middle Ages. And the Middle Ages *were* great, no matter what the sensatists may think about them. To anyone who understands the Middle Ages and who can see beyond his own limited modern sensate tests of value, the Middle Ages are one of the truly great periods of Western man. It is, in fact, quite certain that in most respects the two best societies of Western man have been his two great civilizations resting on spiritual tests of value, Ancient Greece and the Middle Ages. Sensate Rome and the modern world have also been very great civilizations when viewed at their best. Our modern society should not be judged and condemned solely on its standards in its present decadence. But a spiritual civilization invariably has more potentialities for real greatness than a sensate one for the reason that the uplift of the spirit to divinity, the spiritualization of life, give a much higher challenge to man than the concentration of his attention upon the earth-earthy, on the immediacy around him. A sensate civilization by its very nature fetters man to concerns of a lower order. His energies are so much expended upon the delectation of his senses and appetites. He is consumed in the getting, the having, and the enjoying. A spiritual civilization, on the other hand, frees him, challenges him, challenges the best in him, his soul and its great faculties, his will, his intellect, his reason, urges him to soar to the highest realms of which the spirit is humanly capable.

The greatness of the Middle Ages rests in the fact that the spirit of man was lifted to its highest expression, God. Man lived for God, for His Honor and Glory. He wrote his books, his hymns, painted and sculptured his art, built his cathedrals and churches *ad majorem Dei gloriam*. Man was then not an animal, a higher primate as he is in the zoology of today. Still less was he an electron-proton complex, a combination of physico-chemical elements, a reflex mechanism, a variety of stimulus response relationship, a psycho-analytical libido, an organism of glandular activity, a gregarious creature living in somewhat higher and more complicated (*mirabile dictu*) society than ants, bees, and termites as he is defined by some "leading" "scholars" in our decadent physical, social, and psychological sciences of today. Man was a son of God and heir to the Kingdom of Heaven. The stress was on the divine element in man, not the animal or termite element. The heroes of the medieval period were the loftiest and best that man can ever have, God, His Divine Son, the Holy Family, the saints, and holy and virtuous men who by good lives had triumphed over earthly frailty. In its paintings it used the halo to stress the divine in man. As a spiritual society it necessarily put little faith in the visible things of earth and, therefore, in comparison with the pagan world of sensate Rome, which preceded it, it has left relatively few tangible remains of itself outside of its religion, its churches, and its hymns.

What it has left is often supremely good even when judged by sensate standards. The last great medieval man, Dante, has written in the *Divine Comedy* the greatest work of Western world literature, the greatest book of all time, except the Bible. Ruskin, the fine English sensate aesthete, significantly found in Dante "the central man of all the world." The last gasps of the Middle Ages gave the subject matter, and not infrequently the technique, of the greatest art we have had in our history, the first really great art since that of Greece, in the works of Raphael, Michelangelo, and Leonardo da Vinci. The best music of the West is held by great critics to be medieval Gregorian chant. Our greatest art for twenty-two hundred years, the greatest book in all our literature, our best music, these are some of the matters the Middle Ages gave us. If the sensatists are to be aesthetes—and that is part of sensatism at its best—and if they are to be lovers of the best in books, and music, and art, they will have to admit the greatness of the Middle Ages, even if its tests of value were different from theirs. For lovers of the supremely best often do not need to come beyond the sweep of the Middle Ages into Modern Times. Our supremely best to date frequently ended with the Middle Ages.

On the other hand, even if we are confirmed spiritualists, we should not see in the Middle Ages the summit of all possible perfection. There has been an unfortunate tendency for the past one hundred fifty years, from Romanticism onwards, to look upon the Middle Ages as perfect. This error was heightened during the past century by the overzealousness of converts to Roman Catholicity, Anglo-Saxon converts in particular, to extol the Middle Ages beyond any possible factual justification. Their zeal was understandable, even commendable. But it was extreme and not in vain has the wisdom of the ages and of

51

the Church gently suggested that *in extremis latet periculum*. The overzealous lauders of the Middle Ages were joyous to be freed from some of the materialistic and secularistic error particularly prevalent in Anglo-Saxon lands. Looking to the Middle Ages they found a period in which they correctly enough sensed that they would not have been led astray to live in darkness so many years before they found the light. Closing their eyes to many of the very real defects of the Middle Ages, defects which some rather elementary reading in Chaucer, Langland, Dante, Walter von der Vogelweide, Wolfram von Eschenbach, and French *chansons de geste inter multa alia* would readily have laid bare, they have embarassingly praised the Middle Ages beyond all due. What was praiseworthy in the Middle Ages, the source of their real beauty and greatness, is simply the fact that the medieval world realized rather adequately the truth of God inherent in Christian doctrine and that medieval man rather universally understood what he *should* do, even if often he did not do it at all well. That is, the Middle Ages knew what was most important to know. But in many externals which often marred the truth and beauty underneath they were far from perfect.

They were terribly scarred by the physical impoverishment and unrest which they inherited out of the collapse of the Roman world. The world quakings which seemingly were necessary to jar decadent sensate man loose from the values to which he had clung too long and too greedily and too tenaciously inevitably also purged the medieval world too thoroughly of what it badly needed to supplement its high degree of spirituality. There was such universal impoverishment as often to border on the ugly and bestial. There was a pitiful lack of medical and therapeutical knowledge and even sometimes of sanitation. There was a woefully inadequate approach at general educational facilities until close to the end of the Middle Ages. The old Roman legal system was too fatally shattered in many areas to be of much help to the Middle Ages. The trial by ordeal was a savage mixture of inhuman cruelty and un-Christian presumption upon God to show His hand at beck and call in the world of men. The social system of feudalism was permeated through and through with many intolerable injustices. On the one hand, the feudal system had a deep sense of obligation binding all men and all groups in communal duty, communal responsibility, communal rights under God, an excellence rivalled by no contemporary social or political system. But its well nigh irreparable social cleavages, the frequently sad conditions of the serfs, and above all the unpardonable neglect of the serfs as we approach modern times when human values began to yield to money values, were deplorable in the extreme.

The spiritual society of the dawning centuries can build a far better world than that of the Middle Ages provided the stupidity and blindness and self-complacency of modern man do not force upon the West a dissolution similar to—or even on a much more horrible scale than—the upheavals and quakings which sent the Roman world reeling and crashing in ruin. Our future spiritual world will be a much better world than the Middle Ages if our time would adjust its values properly and put first things first, that is, the things of God, cease to make its sensate objects and power and might and prestige the goals by which it lives. At the same time it could probably preserve what could be good in these objects and power if they were incorporated into a spiritual civilization and employed for the greater honor and glory of God. If our time does not accomplish this, it will be stripped of even the sensate values it prizes and be plunged naked and impoverished and needlessly wretched into its spiritual future, which, in turn, will be horribly marred by the stupid prolongation of the decadency and dissolution of our overripe sensate culture.

The blunt fact is that our sensatists, even the wiser ones, are puerile, even blind, in thinking modern times so great an improvement over the Middle Ages. Both civilizations, the medieval and the modern, have been great, no matter how opposite have been their tests of value. The fact that the sensatists, however, see in the Middle Ages, which *are* great, a period suspect, a dark age, an age of unenlightenment and ignorance, superstition and falsehood, and general unloveliness, is *prima facie* evidence of the incompatibility of the two tests of value, an unconscious record that what seems good and true and right to the one set of values seems bad and false and wrong to the other. The hostility and hatred and misknowledge current in our sensate world about the Middle Ages arises almost solely from the fact that they rested on a set of values quite different from those of the modern world, a set of values which the modern world is unwilling and, to a certain extent, unable to comprehend.

Dark Ages and dark ages

It is not so generally well known in our time, however, that the spiritual medieval world held the brilliant, sensate civilization of Rome to be a Dark Age, a period of ignorance, error, superstition, bestiality, of spiritual famine and soul pestilence. To the medievalist Rome—and he would think the same of modern times—was a period of

54

real, almost unbroken darkness, relieved only by Stoicism and similar austere pagan currents and by the stirrings of nascent Christianity. *His* Renaissance was the first to the fourth century A. D. That was the rebirth of the real and true type of world for him, a spiritual world, such as he dimly knew had once existed in the sets of values established by Moses and Isaias and Jeremiah and the other Hebrew prophets. Rome to the medievalist was a Babylon of greed, passion, power, worldliness, so blinded with the self-sufficiency of its own ignorance and error as to have plunged headlong into its destruction, and to have been impotent to protect itself from the justice of an avenging God, who punished it for its sins of materialism. Rome was the medievalist's favorite example of a civilization which had set its tests of value in perishable images in the midst of darkness: in things, in possessions, in contests and sports and pleasures, in high buildings and machines and aqueducts and dams, in power and wealth and armies and victories, in world controls and treaties and restraints and universal economies, *and which had perished.*

.Rome *proved* to the spiritual and medieval world that the eternal tests of value were the right ones, the material and earthly tests the wrong ones. All about itself the medieval world could see the empty shells of Rome, could in the crumbling Roman ruins hear the hollow echoes of the now lifeless world of darkness. Rome had built its tests of value on objects and things and pleasures, and might and force and power—on the primacy of terrestrial existence, which Jesus had condemned. Jesus was the Way and the Truth and the Life. Rome made for incontestable proof that the Christian, spiritual tests of value were right and the Roman, materialistic, utilitarian tests of value were wrong. To the medieval world Rome was poor

in everything in which it itself was rich and even the little
and insignificant earthly things which Rome had had, its
aqueducts, its colosseums, its apartment houses, its huge
buildings, its fleets, its armies, its gold, its commerce, its
roads, its machines, its victories, its conquests, its economic
and political control over the whole world, all these little
and insignificant things of earth, had been taken from it.
"For he that hath, to him shall be given, and he shall
abound; but he that hath not, from him shall be taken
away also that which he hath." What had the Roman
world been? Jesus had named it bluntly and flayingly: an
adulterous generation, an evil one, a generation of hypocrites and vipers[22], an evil tree which had brought forth
evil fruit, ground that received the seed among thorns,
and the cares of this world, and the deceitfulness of riches,
which had choked it, and it had become fruitless. It had
been sullied by adultery, by sodomy and pederasty, by
divorce and birth control. It had amassed gold and power
and military success. It had exercised economic and political control and established its international police force
over the then known world. It had sent its legions to maintain order everywhere. It had fostered a *pax romana* by
disarming its enemies and policing them so that they could
no longer disturb the economic and political tranquility by
which it hoped to prosper. It had built its bastions and
baths, its villas and its villages, its roads and its ramparts
to the north and south and east and west, in England and
Scotland, in Flanders and France, in Germany and Austria,
in Wallachia and Dalmatia, in Africa and Asia. And what
remained of Rome for the medieval period? A memory
and a language and ruins: a memory of a world resting
on false values and a warning to each man and town and
city and province not to do likewise; a language preserved

in the liturgy and by the clergy of the medieval Christian church; and ruins of a meaningless sensate world, of a dark age truly incomprehensible and foreign to the medievalist.

The medieval period may seem a dark age to modern times. It is doubtful, however, if it seems to the moderns as completely dark a period as Rome did to the medieval world. For to the medievalist the darkness of Rome was so great as to have made it largely miss the most significant chain of events in human history: the Nativity and Life and Ministry of Christ, the Savior. "In Him was life and the life was the light of men; *and the light shineth in the darkness; and the darkness did not comprehend it;* that was the true light which enlighteneth every man that cometh into the world. *He was in the world and the world knew Him not.* He came unto His own, and His own received Him not. But as many as received Him [and few Romans and Jews did], to them he gave power to become the sons of God."

> "In ipso vita erat, et vita erat lux hominum; et *lux in tenebris lucet, et tenebrae eum non comprehenderunt.* Erat lux vera quae illuminet omnem hominem venientem in hunc mundum. *In mundo erat et mundus eum non cognovit.* In propria venit, et sui eum non receperunt. Quotquot autem receperunt eum, dedit eis potestatem filios Dei fieri."

To the medievalist, therefore, the Roman-Judaeo sensate world was so darkened and blinded by error, ignorance, superstition, so steeped in false tests of value that it failed to understand the most transcendental event in human history. It spurned its Savior, mocked and scourged Him, condemned Him to death, crucified Him. In the final irony of its ignorance and blindness and superstition it sealed the tomb of its God and set its ridiculous military power over Him to keep Him buried. Everything for which the medievalist stood mocked at the stupidity of Rome. The Resurrection of Christ was the first important event in *the* Renaissance for the medievalist. His world dated from then on. It triumphed coincidental with the decline of Rome and with the disavowal of the material- istic, utilitarian, sensate tests of value by which the learned and rich and powerful men of Rome, as well as those who were neither learned nor rich nor powerful, had lived.

Our modern civilization would seem just as blind to the medievalists as that of Rome. To them, as Shaw has well said in the introduction to his *Joan,* "we should ap- pear as a drove of Gadarene swine, possessed by all the unclean spirits cast out by the faith and civilization of the Middle Ages, running violently down a steep place into a hell of high explosives."

Notes to Chapter One

1. II Corinthians, IV, 18 and III, 18-20.
2. I Epistle of St. John the Apostle, II, 15-16.
3. Odyssey. VI, 1-103.
4. *Ibid.*, V, 340-493.
5. *Ibid..* V, 103-104.
6. *Iliad,* IX, 499-509.
7. Job, XXXVIII, 2, 4, 12, 36.
8. Isaias, II, 11.
9. Matthew, XXIII, 34.
10. I Timothy, VI, 7-12.
11. I Corinthians, III, 18-20.
12. John, XV, 18-20.
13. II Corinthians, IV, 18.
14. James, II, 14-17.
15. Galatians, V, 16-24.
16. John III, 19-20.
17. John VII, 7.
18. Matthew, VI, 32.
19. Matthew, VII, 8.
20. Matthew, X, 29-31.
21. Luke, XII, 22-31.
22. Matthew, XII, 34, XIV, 7, XXIII, 13-39.

CHAPTER TWO

THE SHADOWS OF JUXTAPOSITION

Creativity versus petrification in a renaissance

IF OUR TWO TYPES of Western civilization are so diametrically opposed to one another as thus to view one another not only unsympathetically but even as mutually dark ages, we need to ask: do the transition periods between the two types of culture have a clear understanding of the sweep of values as a whole? Do the transition periods represent a fusion of the sensate and spiritual? Do the members of transition societies, such as our own, or that of the thirteenth to the sixteenth centuries, or the Roman world of the first to the fourth centuries, or the fourth and third centuries B. C. in Greece, or the worlds of Isaias and Jeremiah, have clear concepts of what is going on in their time? Do they themselves represent an adequate integration of the sensate and spiritual tests of value? The answer to all of these questions is a violent "No!"

Nothing drives home more forcibly the irreconciliability of the two tests of value than the way in which they act in periods of transition from one to the other, that is, periods in which they must exist side by side with one another. The dying culture, instead of fusing itself temporarily with the emerging one, is savage against it, persecutes it, and cruelly tries to stifle its rival, to repress it. Unconsciously, or perhaps consciously, the decadent culture and its members sense that their own time limit has been set. Like an unwilling dying man, the declining culture clings more tenaciously and savagely to life than it does during its healthy and vigorous period.

For this reason periods of transition are veritably infernal, hellish years, real *dies irae,* wrathful, dreadful, horrible times, chaotic, disruptive, volcanic, filled with wars, revolutions, famine, pestilence, cruelty, barbarism, sadistic savagery. They are centuries of persecution, of hate, misery, and suffering. The members of a decadent society instinctively hate the harbingers of the new and are roused to savage fury against them, seeking to destroy them while there is yet time. Those members who represent the dawning world of the future are likewise steadfast to their own tests of value. Consciously or unconsciously they know that the future is theirs and are afraid of nothing, are deterred by nothing. Creativity lies in their hands and they do not need to be savage or cruel to set forward the values of their type of world. Hence, their external acts are marked with tranquility, with confidence, which, at the worst, seem acts of arrogance or madness to those who represent the dying values. The harbingers of the future by their very confidence grate on the nerves of the decadents, who are fired with an unholy passion for destruction and reaction.

Thus, the representatives of the emerging cultures often become martyrs, sacrificed to the blind fury of the decadents, who, lacking all tests of creativity for the future, try to make up for their deficiency by force, and fall more and more into negation and destruction. Hence arise the innumerable cases like Jeremiah, Socrates, Christ, who fall victims to the savage reaction of the decadents.

Transition society tends to cleave itself into two antagonistic camps. During transitions there is undoubtedly less fusion of values than there is during the periods of triumphant ascendency of one or the other cultures. Juxtaposition, far from making for fusion, makes for antagonism between the two types of cultures which are not really fusible. On the other hand, during the ascendency of one or the other cultures, there is always a rather significant number in a society who live rather completely apart from the tests of value of the majority. In the midst of our present sensate world there have been monks and nuns and lay people who have lived very effectively by spiritual tests of value. In the medieval world there were by no means rare cases of those who lived quite thoroughly in the world of the senses. Earlier still in the preceding sensate culture of Rome, there were the austere Catos, there were Stoics, and vestal virgins. In the ascendency of a given culture those who live by values different from those in dominance are more or less condescendingly ignored. They are, of course, not understood; but neither are they persecuted. But, as a culture begins to decline, those who do not live by it become suspect. Later still they are mocked or ridiculed; and in the genuine decline of a period they are real candidates for annoyance or inquisition, for persecution and even death. Not too rarely is their lot exile, the cross, the stake, or the hemlock potion. Probably today the decadent moderns would add also a psychiatrical examination as a new refinement of humiliation for those who build a future which the decadents cannot see.

However, at the same time that they are savage or cruel, the transition periods of Renaissance are also truly great periods of creativity. Both types of culture seem to produce some of their best work in a Renaissance period as if they sensed they are vying with one another for superiority over the minds and hearts of men. The dying culture seems to exert its ebbing strength to the utmost, making all it can out of the last years allotted to it, producing such types as Sophocles, Aeschylos, Socrates, Juvenal, Martial, Dante, St. Thomas, Einstein, men, who seem, as it were, to catch up all the loose threads of their culture and sum them up in one final sunset glory. More forcefully still the new, arising culture is a- work peopling the horizon with a veritable blaze of new light, the torch bearers of the future. Within the space of a few generations the groundwork for a whole millennium is usually laid. Much of the outstanding work in art, in literature, in thought, in philosophy, to which numerous generations of coming humanity will look for inspiration and guidance, is done by the dawning culture within a few decades and frequently within a rather limited geographical area. Men who make the future tests of value for a thousand years often write and think and act and create without contact with one another, even without knowing of one another's existence. They work seemingly in a vacuum until the world explodes and disseminates their labors, sometimes on an almost universal scale. More rarely still, as in the case of two of the more important establishers of the tests of value of our modern world, Boccaccio and Petrarch, they know one another and are mutual sources of inspiration to one another.

The Renaissance periods themselves are not happy either for the decadents or the harbingers of the future in many respects. They are instead grim, miserable, horrible, often a real inferno. They are, however, great.

Greatness and happiness are often incompatible. Transition periods are stupendous, but terrifying. Although their members are able to control by the exercise of their own free will the greatness or the insignificance of their own individual lives, they cannot always seek to be happy except in the sense of belonging to the forces of God and working in harmony with them. Those who know that they are working with the will of God are the only happy ones. Those who seek comfort only are unworthy of the God who created them. Unfortunately, so many members who live in periods of transition and renaissance cannot see enough into the future to know the greatness of their age. They are decadents and see only the woe of the declining world. They lack the vision and the optimism to know where they are being borne. The stress and overtone of their period seem predominantly destruction and dissolution and disintegration: to most thinking members, that is; for those who do not think have no idea that anything important is going on. In such periods all of society is in motion somewhere away from what it has been into something new. But what usually is seen is only the dismemberment, the destruction, not the seeds of creativity of the new. The thinking members of such societies are inclined to be disillusioned, fatalistic, pessimistic; and if they do not think, the members constitute the closed "rotarian" mind which sees everything roseate just around the corner by a mere continuation of the *status quo,* no matter how elusive the corner keeps proving. Few there are among the harbingers of the future and fewer still among the decadents who have the sweep of things. The stress for the thinking contemporaries is upon the upheaval, the chaos, the decline.

Thus, the transition and Renaissance periods, which

are generally several centuries in duration, are noted in history for their wars and revolutions and forced migrations, their misery and persecutions. They are the times of the Greco-Persian wars, of the conflict between the Greek city states, the Peloponnesian Wars, the persecutions of Nero and Diocletian, the invasions of the Germanic tribes, the terrible wars and revolutions of the thirteenth to the sixteenth centuries, the world wars, persecutions the pogroms, exiles, the forced migrations and destruction and disorder of the twentieth century and probably of a century or more to come.

The deadweight of inertia

The fact that it is a new Renaissance is what seems to make our twentieth century such a veritable hell. We have possibly seen only the beginning of the horror to date. Before the stupidly blind, decadent sensate world relinquishes its death grasp upon the values of our time, it will perhaps have to be shaken to its very roots in a mounting crescendo of war and misery and suffering and horror. If this is the way the West gets into its new future, the two warm-up wars of the first half of the twentieth century are, in all probability, relatively gentle preludes to the real tragedy of destruction and death and chaos yet to come.

Undoubtedly it lies within the free will of contemporary man to avoid these horrors. Until they come to pass everyone has the obligation to do all in his power to prevent their coming to pass, to work for a greater understanding of the crisis facing Western civilization and to strive with eager might and main to do all he can to sketch in the outlines of the Kingdom of God. Just as realistically, we must face that modern man has certainly

65

shown no great tendency toward a very judicious use of his free will. Nor in the shadow of his third world war does he seem to have any proper realization of what is at stake. He flatters himself that he has made some minor changes in attitude by his becoming narrowly and chauvinistically "international", that he can now talk gropingly of international police forces and restraints and controls. He does not know that his "internationalism" and his potential *"pax democratica"* are very similar to the "internationalism" and the *pax Romana* of Rome moving well along the slope of its decline. He does not properly sense that his "internationalism" is largely only expedient and pragmatic, that it is based on force and the ephemeral agreements of those who have triumphed by force, that it is an imposition of the will of the stronger on the weaker, of the victor on the vanquished, that it is without justice and unselfish love and Christian charity, without which any internationalism is a mockery, that it is only a *modus vivendi,* a trade and balance of power, an attempt to hold on to what they have on the part of those who are suspicious of one another, and suspicious with reason.

Yet, in even this most inadequate shifting of man to a broader vision there are tiny seeds of hope out of which the future must be made. We must always face the fact that we have to work with what we have, not with what we wish we had. And with the grace of God all things are possible—even to make out of the vaguest and most confused stirrings of contemporary man something of mighty import for the future. These stirrings are perhaps all we have a right to expect thus early, if only modern man can also realize at the same time that the span allotted for him to grow these seeds with God's grace into something tremendous for the future is measurably short.

Hopeful for the future is the growing emphasis in some quarters upon the sacredness and dignity of man, not principally because he is man, but because he is a child of God and possessor of an immortal soul; the growing emphasis in some quarters upon the brotherhood of man under God; obfuscated though it may often be by an inadequate and even cruel internationalism-imperialism and racialism and talk of Slav and Germanic and Anglo-Saxon blood brotherhoods; a growing emphasis in some quarters upon the essential equality of every human soul before God, regardless of race or color or social or economic rank, and the corollary emphasis upon the need for such equality among men. Like the emphasis upon the brotherhood of man, this emphasis upon equality is still unclear and muddy, meaning all things to all men, and quite different things to different groups. In its worst form, it is the fond hope and wish of every renegade to see the speedy and revolutionary rise of some universal state which is based upon the complete equality of men and women and the abolition of private property as a fundamental principle, a state in which neither any distinctions of nationality nor the authority of parents over children, nor of public authority over citizens, nor of God over man is acknowledged. Yet, the emphasis upon a new and equitable order is potentially rich in spiritual harvest for the future, if and when it divests itself of its rabble rousing materialism with which it is now almost universally clothed, if and when it becomes a moral principle and ceases to be political fly paper by which to fasten the votes of the unwary, if and when it ceases to be a putch for complete, leveling universal equality aiming at the destruction of most that is noble in the nature and accomplishments of man. Hopeful is the growing emphasis in some quarters upon the need for absolute standards of truth, unswerving morality, absolute justice; the growing emphasis in certain quarters upon a more just economic and social order in which all men consider it an inalienable right to have an equitable share in the goods and wealth which God destined for all men, not just a selfish few. Hopeful is the mounting wave of resentment against the inherent wickedness of the old sensate bourgeois system, in which some had so much and others so little—a movement which is unfortunately so frequently obfuscated with the even greater and more shameless materialism of communism, which sees as the final end and principal destiny of man his sharing in the materialistic goods of earth with no insight at all into the fact that his physical wellbeing should be only a stepping stone to his spiritual growth and the attainment of his true final end—Heaven. Hopeful is the growing emphasis in some quarters upon the need for a more just and adequate peace, for universal justice for friend and foe; the growing emphasis almost everywhere for greater honesty between nations; the timid emphasis in limited quarters for the establishment of the proper moral bases for world peace to replace the outmoded sensate concepts of economic or political bases of peace, balance of power, alliances and counter alliances, world police force, and the big stick.

Most of these emphases are, as yet, unclear. Some are downright obfuscated. A few are still at the present moment potentially as much a force for evil as for good. But the general signs and trends are unmistakable. The forces and men and ideas in our time are adequate to lay, at least, the foundations, the first humble sub-structure for a new spiritual civilization. They are adequate for the needs of their time, which are simply to break the ground and lay the foundations for the future, even if they are at present unprepared to build the more glorious super-structure of a great spiritual civilization which must be the work of generations yet to come. Of doing more than the beginnings our men and our forces and ideas are, doubtless, as yet incapable. They are capable, however, of doing what is required of them: namely, start the twentieth century into a new spiritual culture.

Only one difficulty remains, and that the mighty one: namely, very few people realize that our present civiliza-tion must undergo the most thorough transformation of tests of value which it has yet experienced in its three mil-lennia of existence. The masses of population in the Western world do not yet want to admit the necessity of such a revolutionary transition. They wilfully refuse to admit that the world is exploding about them. It is in this deadweight of inertia, of reactionary materialism, and no where as reactionary as in many of those areas which by slanderous prostitution of language call themselves "lib-eral", that makes us pause and ask if the first half of the twentieth century has taught us anything adequately. It has taught us beginnings doubtless, at least signs of begin-nings. But realistically the picture does not look roseate for the immediate future unless man gets mightily at work implementing the graces of God.

Attempts at reprieve through an imperium mundi

The major nations of the world emerging from their second Great War in the first half of the twentieth century by their actions and attitudes quite honestly admit their lack of confidence in "internationalism" and "peace". They prepare for war at the same time they talk of peace. At the very same moment the air is filled with peace plans and proposals for leagues of international "cooperation" and "peace" enforcement, the same nations which mouth most loudly for peace openly and shamelessly prepare for war. Nations which never before had vast military programs burden themselves with martial expense vaster than the most war minded nations a generation past. Our Western youth which, had it been born a generation earlier, would have enjoyed in major nations a great possibility of avoiding military service and spending its life in the pursuits of tranquility, now everywhere faces universal conscription in those periods of truce which is the closest the modern world ever gets to peace. The nations and peoples of the world live in fear and suspicion of one another. The allies and friends of yesterday are the savage enemies of today, tearing at each other's throats, draining out one another's life blood. The treaties and agreements signed are unconsciously or consciously admitted to be worthless scraps of paper. There is no principal nation in the West which may not justly be accused of having vitiated in fairly recent history either the letter or the spirit of its international pledges. Not infrequently nations shamelessly and flagrantly vitiate *both* the letter and the spirit of their pledges. It is no great wonder, therefore, that even the mightiest look to arms. They follow the patent and inevitable logic of their own low moral tenets. It is not that they hope to preserve peace by their formidable paraphernalia and panoplies of war. They hope, but not too realistically, by them only to survive somehow the first furious onsets of the next war long enough to gather their energies for a more protacted struggle for existence.

Accordingly, the nations try to maneuver themselves into positions of relative security and inaccessibility by swallowing up the states and islands and lands about them, trying to remove themselves as far as possible from the first wounds of conflict, a gesture that is so impotent and futile in a world where distance is rapidly dwindling into insignificance through the conquests of space by the machines and instruments of man. The nations and men of of the West pursue a will-o'-the-wisp; they seek security where there is no security; they fight for peace by war. They fear one another, are jealous of one another. They have in common their fear and little else. They can unite only in war and only as long as the self-interest of preservation from other enemies dictates a martial cooperation. Once the danger is removed, no one is certain of the other, and each falls back upon his own strength, not at all sure that its today's allies will not be its tomorrow's foes. In this century of world wars and the imminence of war it has become clear that the last gasp of materialistic life and security for which our dying sensate culture may hope comes contradictorily enough through war itself. War, and particularly modern war, which is the destroyer of the values by which sensate man lives, destroyer even of his home, his place of employment, the source of his food, in short, his most elementary sensate security, has become also the last means by which he hopes to guarantee a minimum of security to himself. In the *sauve-qui-peut,* devil-take-the-hindmost chaos of our disintegrating sensate world, the real final stake is an *imperium mundi.* Blind sensate man seeks to purchase a reprieve from the death sentence passed against his sensate culture, which, in fact, is already being carried out against it. He seeks the momentary and illusory stability of an Indian summer before the stark reality of the chill of winter in which he is a-shiver. And he seeks this Indian summer of reprieve

71

before the harshness of his winter by imposing his rule upon the world. That is the real final stake which is being played for in the world wars of our upheaval, the rule over all the world. The gamble, begun in the nineteenth century, continues into our day, and will probably outlast the present century. We are playing for the same final stakes for which the decadent sensate Roman world played: the imposition of our will upon the world in the delusion that such a condition can preserve a security and a creativity which are fast slipping from our grasp. This end process will mark the transition from the former sensate world of nationalism to the exploding sensate world of supernationalism—now euphemistically called "internationalism"—then group imperialism, world imperialism, the strong fist of the mighty, and, at last, of the mightiest. Nor will the *imperium mundi,* to whomever it may fall, be it to Anglo-Saxondom, or Russia, or China, or India, or elsewhere, preserve the sensate world from further disintegration and dissolution, anymore than the *imperium mundi* of Rome could save the Roman world from similar dissolution. It will only have prolonged the agony of transition from the sensate culture to the spiritual one. It will only have rendered more chaotic and infernal and terrible the last miserable decades of sensate man.

The parturition of a new world

Of all this the modern westerner in the midst of his New Renaissance has almost no inkling. He has no comprehension of his time as a period of decadency for those values which he is trying so savagely to defend now that they have lost their *élan* of creativity and are honestly not worth fighting for. Still less does he know what type of future is in motion, of what nature our New Renaissance is, or even that he is in a New Renaissance. He is so actively engaged in adjusting some minor prop, tightening some imagined bolt, in his sensate, financial, economic, political world that he cannot see that the whole structure is disintegrating and that frequently the very bolt he tightens, the prop he buttresses, throws strain somewhere else, that instead of preventing or eliminating the collapse, he is actually accelerating it. Modern society is so blind in clinging to its decadent sensate world that it does not know that the world which it is stupidly defending is the exact opposite in tests of value of the one which is being born. The modern world does not realize that instead of the peace and prosperity and comfort for their own sake for which it is so passionately eager it is inheriting the whirlwind. Modern western man, and especially his "leaders" and "experts" and busy-bodies, does not realize that he is giving his attention to everything except the most important matter, the tests of value pleasing to God.

Our age is blind to its realities just as all other Renaissance periods before it have been blind; and in this respect it resembles the previous Renaissance periods so much, especially the two closest to it, the last Renaissance, that of the thirteenth to the sixteenth century, and the last Renaissance of the spirit, that of the first to the fourth century A. D. in Rome.

The very scenes of the last Renaissance are already proving quite prophetic of the scenes of the present one. A person living in the transition period of Italy of the last Renaissance of six hundred years ago would feel quite at home, for example, in many of the scenes of the New Renaissance Italy of the twentieth century. It might even be almost impossible for him to believe he had been dead for six hundred years if he examined only the external events of his native Italy in the 1940's and did not examine too closely the details of the world about him and notice the changed tests of value by which men live, remark that what was then being born is now dying.

For six hundred years ago too Italy was in a period of political upheaval, of revolution, of foreign invasion. In the mid fourteenth century one might have found the English and the Germans fighting up and down the Italian countryside. The leader of the English mercenaries was John Hawkwood. He and his Essex yeomen, the equivalent of General Alexander and his British-American troops of our time, about six hundred years ago ousted the Germans and pushed them slowfully and painfully back toward the north. The Germans made it a veritable *dies irae* for the cities and countryside as they were driven northward. Italians were divided in their sympathies. Some were fighting on the side of the English, some on the side of the Germans. Most of them were sullen non-participants, praying for peace and eagerly wishing that both the Germans and the English would go home and leave Italy to its destiny. France, Italy's leading sister country of the last Renaissance, likewise suffered in its transition centuries under the heel of an invader and was divided in itself.

It was, however, not the military events of the last Renaissance which were of prime importance. Men of the time often, of course, thought that the military events were of prime importance, that the victories or defeats for their individual sides permanently advanced or retarded the cause of "truth". But this is the rôle which blindlings always play, to be tragically uncomprehending of the world about them, of the world in the past of them, of the world in the future of them. The military events of six hundred years ago had, of course, a certain limited importance, just as do those of our own time. But the military events then, as those of our century, were simply part of a much vaster pattern. The most important fact of six hundred years ago was the situation that a new Renaissance was already a full century in motion, that there was being born a change in the tests of value by which men live, that in France and Italy in the midst of an age of invasion and political upheaval were at work the forces of the future, the men and the ideas that were to represent and symbolize and establish the tests of value of the dawning world. All the chaos which was so obvious was the travail of the parturition of the new world and the death agony of the old. Such was the element in which flourished the dynamic forces of the next centuries.

Both France and Italy in their miseries and in their weakness were leading the world. The men who were really creating the future were a-work in the Romance lands: Boccaccio and Petrarch, two of the most important fathers of modernity; Giotto and Marco Polo; and beyond them Da Vinci and Villon and Rabelais and Giordano Bruno and the many other figures, great and small, known and unknown, harbingers of the sensate, pagan, materialistic modern world. Even in far away "barbarous", backward England, the fourteenth century was to produce Wycliffe and Wat Tyler, John Baconthorpe, William Ockham, and William Lagland and Chaucer; and in Bohemia there was Hus.

With the exception of our own time no age has probably been more wretched and miserable, more unhappy, more savage, more cruel than the last Renaissance. With the exception of our own time probably never has the lot

75

of countless millions of people been more chaotic, more unsettled, more disrupted. In the Italy of Boccaccio and Petrarch there were the pestilences and famines of 1340, 1344, and 1348. Florence in 1340 saw fifteen thousand of its inhabitants die from a plague brought on by civil war. There were executions and counter executions, trials for treason and counter trials. Merchants were paid in valueless fiat money of the invading forces. Boccaccio (*Amorosa Visione*) says that Florence was laid under "as many slavish laws as she had citizens". Liberty became the exile and innumerable anxieties took her place. The people regardless of their class or position scarcely dared voice their thoughts. One of the Florentines who did, old Bettone Cini, had his tongue torn out in such a way that he died of it. The Italian cities would one month appoint themselves a leader only to overthrow him the next. Like our own twentieth century contemporaries, with their faith in the "strong man" to solve their troubles, they pendulated twixt Caesarism and anarchy.

The Renaissance scene in Florence on the Feast of St. Anne, July 16, 1342, resembled in its fury the savagery of many a European city in its New Renaissance six hundred years later. The crowd was in uproar against its leader, Walter of Brienne, whom by its own free choice it had invited as its ruler a few months before. The mob besieged his palace, forced his abdication, demanded that he throw his governors to them. These were Baglioni of Perugia, Cerrethieri Besdomini, and William of Assisi. The latter was present with his son, a handsome lad of sixteen, who had no part in politics. Walter, according to the wishes of the mob, gave them William and his son. The people satisfied their fury more gleefully upon the innocent victim than upon his father. In the square of the

Commune, they tore him and his father to pieces and ate the pieces, a scene rivalling in its sadistic cruelty that in which a Roman anti-Fascist mob did to death in the summer of 1944 an innocent citizen accused of being a Fascist.

Morelli, who sounds like a chronicler from the recent Nazi occupation of Europe, in describing the chaos and misery of the times, said:

> "We lived on herbs and reeds, and very bad they were; all the country was full of people who went about feeding on grass like beasts and thus became pre-disposed to contract diseases, nor was there any help for this."

Companies of adventurers, mercenaries, and invaders roamed up and down the countryside from one end of Italy to the other. The malcontent and unemployed formed into armies which became the terror of Italy, appalling even the various political leaders whom they served. As early as 1343, one German *condottiere* had assembled the "Great Company" and had set a standard for frightfulness by blazoning on his breast that he was the enemy of God, of pity, and of mercy. Naples was as sorely assaulted by the rival armies in 1343 as it was in 1943, an exact six hundred years later, almost to the day. King Lewis of Hungary far and wide in Italy slaughtered and tortured the unresisting peasants. His captains, always out of hand, in so far as they wished to risk the plague of the cities and the earthquakes of Naples, alternated the pleasures of loot and murder with those of rape. And above all the plague, fed by the chaos of war and revolution and the accompanying malnutrition, was the common leveler. It ravaged all Europe. In Avignon it numbered among its prey popes and cardinals. Whole villages lost every inhabitant. In Florence in 1348 it claimed six out of every ten citizens. In Ravenna and Pisa and Siena seven out of eight perished. At Trapani not a soul survived.

The newly emerging wealthy groups of the arising sensate future were for a moment jarred back into the abandoned medieval past. They laid their gold on church altars to clear themselves of guilt and placate heaven, or they threw it over the walls of convents, whence the convent dwellers hurled it back as contaminated and useless. The charitable Or San Michele was overflowed from donations of terror. Just as in the war-pestilence-malnutrition ridden Europe of the Renaissance of today there were six hundred years ago in the last Renaissance license and looting and callousness in contrast to religious fear and attempts at atonement and placation. Sensatism and spirituality existed side by side without fusion as studies in opposites.

The horrors of pestilence, however, seemed only for the moment worse than those of the almost constant wars. Petrarch, one of the comparatively rare men of his century who really understood the change in values going on in his time and comprehended the forces of the future, could not help being shocked by the horrors of the wars. He fretted at the invasion of the East Anglians and the Germans. His beloved Lombardy was seeing Englishmen in numbers for the first time. That fecund father of modernity, seeing John Hawkwood and his Essex yeomen, began to understand how the victories at Crécy and Poitiers had come about, at the same time that he cursed the barbarities of the English and the Germans. He saw the armies of both dancing about their bonfires on the hillsides of Fiesole, shouting insults at each other and at the city below. Like the rest of Tuscany he believed that the "Latins must always hold the Germans in enmity, seeing that we are opposed to them in act and deed, in manners and soul; not only is it impossible for us to serve, but even to hold intercourse with, that race." He was almost as indignant against the English, holding them a "barbarous race, who know naught of beauty, but who would sell their soul for a florin."

It was under circumstances very similar to those under which the Badoglio government declared war against the former Italian ally, Germany, in 1943, that Petrarch wrote the stirring lines urging Florence and Naples and Ravenna to take up arms against the Czech and Hungarian and German invaders from the north:

> "Virtù contra furore
> Prenderà l'arme; e fia 'l combatter certo,
> Che l'antico valore
> Nell' italici cor non è ancora morto."

These lines were quoted throughout Italy during the chaos of 1943 as they were almost six hundred years ago in the chaos of the last Renaissance.

The similarity of the twentieth and fourteenth centuries as times of war and upheaval, murder, rapine, savagery, and cruelty is striking. The eventual goals of the two periods, one into a world of the senses, the other into a world of the spirit, are quite different. But to a limited outlook, stressing only the chaos of transition, the similarity is startling.

Almost everywhere six hundred years ago the old, medieval spiritual civilization was breaking up. Italy was particularly interesting because in the midst of foreign invasion and terror it was leading the last Renaissance. Religious division and modern materialistic standards were beginning to sully the Church's bosom. Waves of social

79

disturbance, augmented by pestilence and war, passed through all of Western civilization. The agrarian feudal order was giving way to urban industrialism and commercialism, to bourgeois capitalism, to political nationalism, stays of the modern sensate order. In Flanders, in France, in Switzerland, in England even, the peasants were on fire with the changing world. In 1356—the year of Poitiers—occurred the first rising of the Jacquerie in France. Before the Wat Tyler upsurge in England there was the Ciompi rising in Florence.

In the midst of all this chaos of pestilence and famine and war and revolution, however, in the conflict between the dying world of the past and the nascent sensate world of the future, the societies as a whole, representing the two opposite tests of value, had no understanding of their time as a period of transition, any more than they understood one another. The cleavage between the medievalists and the arising modernists was almost complete. Their hatred of one another, their inability to comprehend one another, was one of the causes of the prevailing chaos. In the same land one group, one area, belonged to the past, another to the future. There was no fusion of the two worlds, only confusion. Contrast and opposition of values were in the air. The atmosphere was filled with the sensate future, but the spritual past strove vainly to hold it in check. Boccaccio and Petrarca, however, knew where the future lay. Side by side they disinterred and deciphered the classical codices which were to help overthrow Christian altars by spreading the gospel of the senses. They invented such sensate cultural slogans as knowledge for knowledge's sake and art for art's sake. They were consciously and knowingly bringing about changes in the tests of value by which men live. But their societies did not understand the transition. They knew only the chaos, the fact that the dread four horsemen of the Apocalypse were on the earth. The chaos of Europe in our own time which we have thought so terrible is only a bit more accentuated than that of the Renaissance of six hundred years ago. The horror of transition of the last Renaissance and of the present one is startlingly similar.

The periods of Renaissance themselves, thus, represent no fusion between the two opposite tests of value. The hostility between them, rather, is accentuated and they are never more irreconciliable than at times when one set is dying and the other springing to birth. The decadent is savage, cruel, sadistic, repressive, retro-active, destructive, reactionary, even anarchic and nihilistic. The new is confident, unyielding, uncompromising. Compromise in anything as basic as tests of value is the way of cowards and of the groping and uncertain. There is never anything uncertain about an emerging new test of value. It is one of the most certain forces in the world. The future for the next millennium belongs to it.

Renaissance studies in opposites

What of the persons themselves in the Renaissance periods? They too like the societies to which they belong fall usually into sharply cleft groups. In periods of transition forced extremes of type are likely to prevail. This is necessarily so. The harbingers of the future, until the Renaissance is well advanced, are necessarily small in number. They concentrate in themselves the vitality, the creativity of the future. They sum up, represent, symbolize, carry within themselves the various currents of the next thousand years. They are explosive with the ideas of the world to come, dynamic with potentialities which it will realize. It may happen, however, that they are not very conscious of what forces they represent. They are confident, often only dimly knowing why they are so. In the last Renaissance Boccaccio and Petrarca were the exceptions rather than the rule. Even they, especially Boccaccio in his final years, did not entirely understand that they were helping to found a new world and destroy an old.

Even less do the decadents—and they inevitably make up the majority of the membership in the early decades of a Renaissance world—know what is going on. They unconsciously sense a change; and because they sense a change against the world they represent, they savagely cling to their world, try to defend it to the death, tenaciously grasp what is slipping from them. This tenacity of defense inevitably identifies them with reaction. The majority of the defenders of a passing world end by being stiflers and repressionists, if necessary to the point of persecution. Hence, arise those striking contrasts of spirituality and sensatism in the periods of transition, contrasts which are beginning to be so prevalent in our time and with which unquestionably future generations will also be filled. The chaos and calamities of the times affect various individuals in quite different ways. The Renaissance makes saints and martyrs out of some whose nobility and courage of soul are exemplary and symbolical sources of inspiration to their weaker contemporaries and to the generations to come who will call their memory blessed. It makes criminals and reprobates out of others and drives them into acts of animalism and savagery and cruelty which to call bestial would shame and insult the beasts to which they might be compared.

Most members of transition periods, however, are not extremists. They remain simply dull and uncomprehending of their times. They do not know what is going on, have no realization of the fact that one world is dying and another is springing to birth. They are absorbed in the calamity and misery and chaos on the one hand; or else they remember wistfully and pine for the "normalcy" of "the good, old days", a normalcy which will never return. In this respect the dominant note of every Renaissance period is uncomprehension, to the point of stolidity, of the forces at work in the world.

Our own Renaissance to date is in this respect no exception to those of the past. There is a very considerable number of the leaders of thought and action this past century who belong in a very positive way to the dawning world of the spirit. No small number of them have had deep insight into the nature of the world they have been helping to create: the recent Popes, Dostoievski, Berdyaev, Sorokin, Baudelaire, Rimbaud, Péguy, Gilson, Claudel, Jammes, Maritain, DeGaulle, Newman, Belloc, Chesterton, Dawson, Sheen, Hutchins, Koestler, Fr. Keller, Werfel, Borchhardt, and many others. Yet, in spite of the unquestionably clear insight into the needs of our time by a large number of men, the over-all picture is one of dull, wilful incomprehension. Understanding of the nature of our time is probably at lowest ebb in those nations where the cult of materialism has the most unquestioning devotees, Russia and America, for example, where there is still an almost unshaken faith in material progress, in objects and gadgets, in machines and engines, in science and secularism, in one's own unconquered might. Understanding is probably a trifle better in Germany, an additional trifle still in England, and seemingly best of all in France and Italy, apparent leaders of the present Renaissance as they were those of the last. But even in France and Italy the emphasis is unfortunately too frequently still on materialism, not spirituality, not only among the masses of people, but equally so among the leaders and "intellectuals".

For every Sorokin and Dostoievski and Berdyaev, for every Werfel and Borchhardt and Lowenstein, every Péguy and Claudel and Maritain, every Hutchins and Adler and Sheen there are literally thousands upon thousands of blindlings who do not know that we are ankle-deep in a New Renaissance, that we are replacing the centuries old sensate values of the modern and Roman worlds again with the spiritual ones of ancient Greece and the Middle Ages. And in their blind stolidity they are likely to consider as most suspect any one who tells them of the truth of their time.

In between the blindings on the one hand, who are not conscious of the currents of their world, and the extremists of the nascent future or of the dying past on the other, there is a small but interesting group who do frequently approximate being fusionists of the two tests of value. They are, indeed, *rarae aves,* almost engulfed by the blinder majority unconscious of their time, and also scarcer and less active, and, therefore, less conspicuous than the extremists of the past and future. These are the "expressionist" types, Spengler, Shaw, Bernstein, Turgenev, Bergson, Ortega y Gasset. They sense and express their pessimism, their delusion, even their disgust, at the present decadence, but they are not enough of the future to belong really and creatively and positively to it. Here belong, especially in literature and art, the satirists who flay a decaying order but who comprehend so little of the new. Here belong also those limited visionaries, certain types of intellectuals, who sense vaguely, even uncomfortably, that the old order changeth, but who never quite get to understand the nature of the change. They are the Renaissance group most to be pitied. They remind one of that group of neutral angels so well described by Dante in the third canto of the *Inferno*. Because they had remained neutral in the rebellion of Lucifer against God, Heaven cast them forth and Hell would not receive them; so they were condemned eternally to be blown impotently twixt Hell and Heaven. This group is truly pitiful, fortunately small. Here belong such Roman satirists and philosophers as Juvenal, Martial, Petronius, Marcus Aurelius; among the limited visionaries of our time such a potentially great figure as Prime Minister Jan Christian Smuts of the Union of South Africa; less certain still because they are still too shrouded in the obfuscation of contemporary history, but definite potentialities as limited visionaries, Petain, Sartre, Toynbee, Mussolini, Wilkie, Wallace, MacArthur, Tolstoi. The Roman satirists were pitiful because, understanding so much of the decadence of Rome, they caught nothing of the future. A man like Smuts in our time is pitiful, sensing so well the change of the old order but, seemingly, yet, at least, not comprehending the nature of the new. Several years ago he was quoted as saying after the Cairo Conference among Churchill, Chiang-Kai-Chek, and Roosevelt:

"Something is shaping into a vision of the future. . . . Elements are gathering for something bigger than was ever dreamed of in human history. We can only hope that the indescribable suffering will not be in vain and we will reap their fruits."

Here belong in most instances our expressionist artists and writers and the surealists and existentialists, all consciously or unconsciously in revolt against such end-of-the-century

85

decadence as naturalism and impressionism, groping for forms in which to express their revolt, yet cognizant in no way that they are transition figures into a new society of the spirit. In a literary sense they may be among the most outstanding figures of their age. Such certainly are Spengler and Shaw and Sartre.

The expressionists like Ortega y Gasset, the limited visionaries like Smuts, the satirists like Juvenal, and the really creative harbingers of the future like Giotto or Petrarch, or John the Baptist and St. Paul, or Dawson or Péguy or Belloc are in any period of transition a very small part of the total membership in a Renaissance society. Their effect may be offset for generations, even centuries, by the numerically more powerful elements, the reactionary extremists and the most numerous blindlings. Our population living now in the New Renaissance of the Spirit in spite of the stupendous potentiality for the quick exchange of ideas *via* radio and telegraph, cinema and television, newspaper and books certainly makes no exception to the stolidity and petrification characteristic of transition eras. It is with us as it was with ancient Rome. The sensate world is decaying. The decline of Rome is more or less literally repeating itself before our eyes. A new world of the spirit is springing into birth even as the old world of the senses is passing away. And who knows it? Some authors and philosophers and clergymen; a handful of university professors, typified in this country by Sorokin and Hutchins; occasional business men, scientists, lawyers, and other professionals; very rare statesmen like Salazar and DeValera and De Gaulle; and a sprinkling of humble folk who without letters or deep education know more than most of the statesmen and professors of the world.

In a sense, such lack of comprehension would be more understandable if a spiritual society in decay, such as that of pre-Hellenistic Greece or that of the last Renaissance, should fail to heed the signs of the future. A spiritual society is not primarily interested in the earth-earthy and, therefore, conceivably might not understand its peril when confronted with its own decline and the rise of a new test of value. Moreover, a spiritual society instinctively knows its devotion to the things of God is right and, therefore, it stubbornly refuses to relinquish its hold to the materialistic forces whose triumph it comprehends can never be permanent, even if it does seem irresistible at a given moment. But the fact is that our Western spiritual societies in decline, although they understand the future somewhat inadequately, seem far better to understand the Renaissance which destroys them, than do our sensate societies in their sunset, like that of Rome in the first centuries A. D. or our own modern world. The Greek contemporaries of Demosthenes knew something of the impending future. Demosthenes saw, at least, to that. The ecclesiastical inquirers into the ideas of Galileo knew for a certainty that the sensate tests of value and the "truth" which he proposed made for a complete break with the tests of value of divine revelation and spiritual truth of the past.

When his judges read in Galileo's letter to Benedetto Castelli (1613) that he held there is no human or divine authority which may be placed over the authority of experiment and mathematical deduction, when they read in his *Dialogues* his assertions that the verities of mathematics and physics are as immutable as the laws of God, yea more, that, in case of conflict between God's Revelation and the rigid laws of nature ascertained by empirical observation, the balance of "truth" must incline to the latter rather than to the former, they knew that one of the keystones of their spiritual world was giving way. For in their spiritual medieval system there could always be an insurmountable barrier separating the two systems of truth, the truth of God, and truth of men. There was an immanent and a transcendental truth, a human and a divine truth, a truth of reason and of observation, and a higher truth of Revelation. Galileo in his *Dialogues* and in his trial ventured to demolish this distinction. He claimed that man can know mathematical and scientific truth as thoroughly and as perfectly as God, probably not *all* of it, but part of it. Mathematics, he proclaimed, is indivisible. He would admit no immanent or transcendental, no human or divine mathematics. His judges and Pope Urban VIII did not really seriously question the scientific "truth" of Galileo. To a certain extent they even acknowledged the Copernican theory to be an admissible astronomical hypothesis. They did not try Galileo for his scientific assertions. They understood that something was at stake far more important than the assertions themselves. As spiritualists they were wise enough, and correct enough, to understand the significance of Galileo's tests of value. For they maintained that the omnipotence of God is not contingent on the rules and principles of human reason; that God, therefore, was perfectly free to create and establish and guide the world according to laws entirely divergent from those which human science may discover and human reason comprehend. Galileo could not accept this view. He refused to acknowledge any possible contradiction between the will and working of God on the one hand and the axioms of mathematics and the "facts" of physics and of scientific observation on the other. To him "truth" was of the immediate and sensate world, one and indivisible. Galileo's judges understood him perfectly and, without pronouncing on the "scientific truth" or falsehood of his assertions, for they were not interested in it, did as logical and consistent upholders of spiritual and divine tests of value which can, if need be, transcend the faulty observation of men, pronounce Galileo's tests of value and criteria of judgment wrong.

They comprehended the nature of the threat of the future, if his sensate approach to truth by the senses and observation and the immediacy of science were accepted over their spiritual one. They were right from their spiritual point of view. Galileo is unquestionably one of the greatest creators and establishers of sensate truth. But he is wrong, if it is possible that God's ways are not always fathomable to man. Galileo was right if man's knowledge, as far as it goes, is as infallible as God's. It is axiomatic that God's workings will not contradict genuine truth. But just how could Galileo guarantee that his mathematical and physical knowledge was perfect truth? He had nothing more reliable than the faulty methods of empirical science which depend upon observation and experiment, depend ultimately on the provably inaccurate senses and the possibly faulty judgments and interpretations of man. The Christian spiritualist now or in medieval times must hold that God's ways are not necessarily fathomable to man. They may be fathomable in a given instance, or they may not be. It is always possible, however, that they may not be. "Then the Lord answered Job out of a whirlwind. . . . 'Where wast thou when I laid the foundations of the world? Tell me if thou hast understanding.' " Galileo's judges well understood him and his significance. To the sensate world ever since they have stood as symbols of clerical ignorance and short-sightedness, of men in "error". Yet, they were certainly right if the ways of God can be different from the ways of men. But at any rate, compared with the sensatists of our day who understand almost nothing of their time or the impending future, they were clear visioned seers. The worst of which they can be accused is a reactionary defense of a test of value which was unfortunately almost dead. They defended divine truth when the world was not in a mood to hear that God can be greater than man. Interesting also is the fact that they were not savage or cruel in defending their tests of value, for they made only a pretense of "protective custody" for Galileo, gave him almost unhampered facilities for work and comfort, and even some of them, like the Pope, more or less agreed with him in his purely scientific assertions, if he would only allow room for their higher spiritual tests of value, the thing which Galileo would not allow. They were alive to the past and defended it; but they also understood the threat of the sensate future, and logically and correctly as upholders of a spiritual society condemned it. They had far more insight than is possessed by most of our contemporary sensate leaders. For these, cruelly, sadistically, savagely, hold on to the past and deny that there is any future except in their tests of value. Unlike Galileo's judges they fail even to recognize the existence of values opposite to theirs. They, therefore, cannot intelligently condemn them. They are usually not even alert enough to know of them.

Thus, in the midst of our present sensate decline there seems to be no one who has written as understandingly of the future as did Demosthenes for his contemporaries or the judges of Galileo at the time of the dissolution of their respective spiritual worlds. Demosthenes and Galileo's judges gauged better the revolution that the arising

new ideas would bring than men today seem to gauge the
course of our future. The declining sensate worlds are
blinder than the declining spiritual ones to the upheaval
of their time and to the changing tests of value by which
men live. Rome in its sunset and we in ours are the blindings *par excellence* to our time.

Creativity two thousand years ago

At the time of the last transition period like our own,
a transition from a sensate world to a spiritual one, the
rich and powerful men of Rome understood nothing of the
significance of their age. Little more can be said for its
learned men, its historians, its philosophers, its scientists,
its engineers, its inventors, its economists, and educators.
With the exception of its embittered satirists and essay-
ists the rich and influential and learned men of Rome
did not know that their civilization was in decay. Martial
and Juvenal and Petronius and Tacitus, although inadequately comprehending the future, did understand enough
of their time to know that the values by which men lived
were non-creative, outmoded, ridiculous, and they flayed
them vehemently. One is struck with admiration on the
one hand for the great insight of Juvenal or Martial into
the decadence of Rome; one is moved to pity on the other
hand that they were left without one ray of hope, one
iota of understanding of the creative forces of the future.
Like the expressionist authors and painters and musicians
of today they were vibrant with the ferocious intensity of
hate against the decadent present, pulsing with revolt
against its inadequacy. But they remained only forces of
negation like the Van Goghs and the Picassos of our time.
They were creative only in their negation of the decadent

and the impotent. They were not as much creators of the future as garbage collectors of the outmoded past.

Christ, Peter, Paul, John the Baptist, John the Evangelist, Mary the Virgin Mother, Mary the repentant sinner, these and numerous others, both great and small, named and unnamed, were the real leaders of the future in the Rome of Augustus and Tiberius, Nero and Petronius, Martial and Juvenal. They were the leaders of the Christian Renaissance, the last Renaissance of the spirit, the Renaissance that inspired a new life into Western civilization for the next thousand years and took the pagan, materialistic standards of value of decadent Rome and replaced them with a strong and vigorous and creative new set of values of Christian Europe. These new values were to be in turn triumphant until the world of the senses and of the everyday made again its demands in the last Renaissance, pushed the spiritual values once more in whole or in part into the background and established our modern sensate world. These sensate values dominated our West until the middle of the nineteenth century when they began again to fall into decay, lost their creativity, and are now yielding *de novo* to a New Renaissance of the Spirit. Christ, Peter, Paul, Mary the Virgin Mother, Mary Magdalene are again the leaders behind the New Christian Renaissance in our time just as unmistakably as they were in that of the first century A. D. Medieval and modern leaders have of course also arisen and are arising to carry on the work which the founders of Christianity so nobly began, Aquinas, Augustine, Albertus Magnus, Thomas à Kempis, St. François de Sales, Ste. Thérèse de Lisieux, Ste. Bernadette of Lourdes, Péguy, Claudel, Newman, Dostoievski, Dawson, Belloc, Maritain, Pope Pius XI and XII, Sheen, and many other both great and wee folk, who are playing the truly creative rôles of our time and of the future.

Significantly then, almost two thousand years ago, in the last period like our own, the great of Rome, Tiberius and Nero and Seneca and Pliny, its emperors, its arbiters of taste, its great scientists and authors, failed to understand the decadence of their world and even less had any inkling of the future. The decadence of Rome was sensed by a few, by Martial, Tacitus, and Juvenal. But the future was being comprehended—and made—by Christ and those around him.

Centuries in advance of his time the Elder Cato told his fellow Romans what would happen to them if they persisted in their crass materialistic ways. Since at the time of Cato, Rome had not yet reached the highest pinnacle of its sensate creativity and especially since it *preferred* not to listen to him, it conveniently dismissed him as a sour prophet of evil, a needless Cassandra, who knew not whereof he spoke. Both Rome and Cato, each within their proper sphere, had been correct. As a troublesome old man Cato was a grouch. Sensate Rome accordingly disliked him. But he was shrewd enough mixture of militarist, bourgeois, and sensate idealist to see the threat to materialistic creativity in a Rome which wanted to be wealthy, secure, indolent, effeminate, soft. Herein Rome was wrong and Cato right. On the other hand, Cato failed to see that the comforts and culture, the urbanity and cosmopolitanism to which Rome aspired were the very life blood of a creative sensate world as long as such comforts and culture, urbanity and cosmopolitanism were dedicated to what is best in a sensate society. Herein Rome was right and Cato was just a grouch. But grouch or prophet, Cato had no foresight of the possibility of spiritual forces which would one day make his little national capital the spiritual capital of the world.

Along with Cato, Polybius had in politics and statescraft a keen eye for the trends which would lead to the ruination of Rome. Polybius is greatly reminiscent of Oswald Spengler in our time. Like Spengler he had an almost complete insight into the nascent decadence of his age and into the political character which it would assume. Also like Spengler he was so imbued with pessimism that he failed to see that there could be other forces at work which *after* the decadence could build a new sort of world with different tests of value even in the same geographical areas, yea on the very ruins, of the old. Polybius well understood and succinctly described what Spengler in our time calls the movement of "Caesarism", the trend by which self-appointed strong men, selfish and bloated leaders of the masses, conduct around by the nose the countless millions whom they alternately "represent", abuse, wheedle, starve, feed, adulate, and push in and out of war.

"So when they [*i. e.,* the "leaders"] begin to lust for power and cannot attain it themselves through their own good qualities, they ruin their estates, tempting and bribing the people in every possible way. Hence, when by their foolish thirst for reputation they have created among the masses an appetite for free gifts and the habit of receiving them, democracy is abolished and changes into an order of force and violence. For the people, having grown accustomed to feed at the expense of others and to depend for their livelihood on the property of others, as soon as they find a leader who is enterprising . . . institute the rule of violence . . . and for this the populace will be responsible! For on the one hand they imagine that they have a grudge against certain people who have shown themselves over-greedy. On the other hand they are puffed up by the flattery of those who aspire to office. Stirred to fury and swayed by passion in all their undertakings they will no longer consent to obey or even be the equals of the former upper groups but will demand the lion's share for themselves. When this happens, the state will change its name to the finest sounding of all: it will go under the name of freedom and democracy. But it will change its nature to the very worst of all, for it will be the rule of the mob." Polybius, *Histories*, VI, 9 and 57.

Polybius prophetically wrote this thirty years before the time of Caius Gracchus! He caught the *political* trend of Rome for the next three centuries as Spengler has caught our political trends. But he caught absolutely nothing of the spirit which Christ would bring, which would lay hold upon the political upheaval Polybius so well foresaw and save the world from the enduring ruin which he dreaded. Polybius' words will probably sound applicable to many political trends of our present decaying sensate West at frequent times in the twentieth or twenty-first centuries. Like Spengler in our time he foresaw the decline of the West without an inkling of its Renaissance.

Cicero, much closer to the beginning of the final decay in Rome, in fact, at its very threshold, likewise understood the threat of his time and dedicated his life half-unselfishly, half-selfishly in trying to make the Romans see the menace of their future. He was, perhaps, the last important Roman of gigantic historic stature not to belong in some way or other to the decadence, to make it inevitable, to participate in the downward plunge. And with Cicero many of the Stoics sensed the decadent trends of their age and reacted as best they could against them. But neither Cicero nor they held the light of the future in their hand.

It was not, thus, in any of the pagan great of Rome, not even in their clearest, almost prophetic, thinkers, that the real creators of the future were to be found. A few there understood part of their time. But they could not, perhaps in a sense through no fault of their own, participate in building the new tests of value of the future.

95

Through no fault of their own we may say because it was only by grace of a miracle that Paul himself came to see the light.

Miracles can be necessary to make the members of a society realize something of the will of God. The difference between Paul and most of the Roman-Jewish world was the fact that Paul heeded his miracle. But not all his contemporaries could say the same. Many witnessed greater miracles than Paul's and did not believe. Certainly one of the faults of blindlings in a spiritual Renaissance like our own or that of the first century A. D. is the condition that they do not heed their miracles. In the face of Fatima and Lourdes modernity cannot say it lacks its miracles and its exhortations. In face of the Incarnation the Roman world could not say it was not given very special helps to correct its false values and set them aright. It was not, it is true, given the individual, private miracle of the Road to Damascus. In a vaster sense, however, it was given much more—it was given the vastest chain of miracles the world has ever seen, in the Birth and Ministry and Crucifixion of its Savior.

The builders of the future in the decaying sensate Rome of almost two thousand years ago were the Christians. The real leaders, although few recognized them as such, were Jesus and Peter and Paul and John and all the others who by 90 A. D. had said or written what were to be the standard tests of value for the next one thousand years. The builders of the future values were not to be found among Rome's "chief citizens", her emperors, her financeers, her lawyers, her engineers, her educators, economists, actors, playwrights, and still less, among her favorite prostitutes, cunnilambentes, fellatores, fellatrices, gladiators, charioteers, and rabble rousers. Those who built the future were the spiritual figures, whatever their rank or class or degree of wealth, from slave to fisherman, from physician to senator, who came to accept the way of Christ. It is true that the names of the great and influential men in Rome were missing from the Christian spiritual leaders of the Renaissance of the first century A.D. There was not a single Roman headliner among them. But the Christian leaders of the future were definitely not all poor and ignorant men and women without sensate and materialistic capabilities and potentialities. There was learning among them (Luke was a physician); there were successful and wealthy men and women among them. Joseph of Arimathea, Zachaeus, and Nicodemus are, for example, New Testament proofs of rich men who in loving and following Christ and in spreading His gospel were builders of the future and its tests of value. The great cities of the Mediterranean world, and above all, Rome, saw from the first century onward a fair number of rich men and women join the small group of Christian formers of the future. There were also humble folk, fishermen, carpenters, slaves, albeit an infinitesimal fraction of the whole population of Rome and its world empire, who were a-work establishing the spiritual values by which the coming generations were to live for the next millennium.

Christianity and the making of the future did not belong to one class or rank or profession or stratum of society except to the extent that the real "headliners" did not begin to join until it was a most thriving concern. Both those sensately rich and sensately poor created the future almost two thousand years ago. The important thing is that both its rich and its poor creators understood that the materialistic, utilitarian, sensate values were outmoded, that the world was sick and needed to be born anew. They had the grace of creativity to set about building the new world of spirituality in values of the soul, of human sanctity, of God, of eternity.

Creativity today

It is much the same case now in our similar Renaissance almost twenty centuries later. The challenge is laid down to all men to become creative participators in it. No man alive today can escape the challenge. Neutrality before the challenge is impossible. Those who try to be neutral convict themselves. The times demand positive participation in the building of the values of the Kingdom of God. Those who refuse such positive participation become automatically forces of negation. When God's Kingdom is at stake, it is really true that those who are not with Him are against Him. Indifferentism is in many ways the most negative of attitudes before the Kingdom of God. Yet, the universality of the challenge to modern men to become workers for the Kingdom of God does not mean that the challenge is universally accepted. Nor is the opposite the case: neither is it universally rejected. As in the similar world of two thousand years ago the challenge is accepted by some, unfortunately rejected by others.

There are not many of our "headliners" who are playing creative rôles for the future. With unfortunately too few exceptions, such as Werfel and Dostoievski, who are themselves transitional figures belonging both to the sensate past and the spiritual future, the creators of the future are usually not found among the names of recent modern or contemporary authors of international "best sellers". Yet the future *is* in motion. Some few people do understand their time and are playing its creative rôles,

perhaps one person in ten thousand. As in the first century
A. D. they will be found among all classes and ranks.
There will be scientists and writers and physicians and
professors and wealthy and successful men among them.
There will be the poor and ignorant and the conquered
and enslaved among them. All will, however, be bound
together by a common bond—that of spirituality. They
will understand that the world is sick and needs to be
born anew. They will comprehend that the tests of value
which rest on the primacy of life, on material possessions,
on things, sensations, comforts, luxuries, security, earth-
earthy reality, navies, armies, air-fleets, international economic ententes, world police forces, financial stabilizations,
materialistic distributivism, enforcement of the laws and
will of the stronger, to the extent that any or all of these
are not rooted in God, are not the creative tests of value
by which men are to live, that such forces are outmoded,
decadent, and that they must and will be discarded; painfully and chaotically discarded, if necessary, that is, if
man by his free will makes the wrong choices, intelligently
and with confident and prophetic insight if the free will
of man will only choose aright. But they will be discarded
at any rate to make way for the new creative spiritual
world of the future, a society basing its tests of value on
human sanctity, the soul, in God, and in eternity.

The builders of the future must likewise be marked
by one other most important sign, the most important of
all—the Love of God. It is Love of God that must permeate the world anew. Love of God is the purest and
most genuine stuff out of which the future can be made.
The humblest and most nameless and most illiterate folk
of our time who love God are literally more alive to creative participation in building the world of the future than

the leaders of nations, than men with great international reputations, than learned professors in supposedly respectable institutions of erudition, if the leaders of nations, the headliners, and the learned professors do not love God. It is the Love of God which has been most sadly lacking in the poor pitiful world of the past. Man for these many centuries past has been thinking he could get by with lip service to God, even an unwilling lip service at that, given begrudgingly. Poor fool! Without Love of God even the best of worlds will decay.

The Love of God is a most intangible thing, and yet very tangible. It cannot be measured by the learned instruments of measurement which our psychologists and educators and sociologists and scientists evolve for the measurement of almost anything in the universe. Yet, it is so tangible that it must infuse itself into the very essence of creation. All creation must by necessity in duly ordered ways love and serve its God. Only man is free to rebel. When he rebels, the whole world goes all awry, and in very tangible fashion. An onion is not free to rebel against its God. An onion must love and serve and honor God in its own pre-determined, simple fashion. An amoeba, tiny, humble creature of God, is bound by duty in its own tiny, humble way to love and honor and serve its Creator. And so on, until we come to great man. He too, creature of God, is bound to love and honor and serve his Creator. When he does not, he sets the world all topsy-turvy, strikes at the security of homes, the life, the food, the very existence of man everywhere throughout the world today. Love of God is the very tangible stuff out of which order and harmony exist. Love of God is the very tangible stuff out of which the new world must be built. Love of God is the mark of any creative spirit of our time.

Hand in hand with Love of God, inseparably bound up with it, is love of man. For on each man is imprinted the indelible mark of God. Each man partakes somewhat of the nature of God. Each man has a soul and is a candidate for participation in the Mystical Union with the Body of Christ. We cannot love God adequately nor truly unless we also love our fellow man. And we cannot truly love our fellow man without loving most in him the handiwork of God.

Finally, the stuff out of which the future is made must be love of the attributes of God—Beauty, Truth, Justice, Hope, Kindness, Goodness, Mercy. Slowly, the Poet or the Lover who seeks after beauty in our time may come to understand that in loving some earthly form of beauty he is really seeking and thirsting for the Source of all Beauty. Those who seek after justice, who thirst for justice so intensely in our modern world with its many injustices, may slowly come to be builders of the future on the Justice of God even if they have so little idea of either what or how they are to do, even if passion blinds them yet so that they are still unable to see the Source of all Justice. And so on: Truth, Hope, Kindness, Goodness, Mercy, they are all too the stuff out of which the future must be built.

Yet, today there is everywhere so little realization of this among so many, but at the same time so keen a realization of it among some. To the spiritual thinker of coming centuries, a true brother to the medievalist, our time will offer a striking parallel to the time of Christ and Peter and Paul, of Tiberius, and Nero and Juvenal. It will be seen that our influential and powerful men, shepherds of the people, our leaders and führers and presidents of nations are often understanding much too little of the significance of our time. Not much more will be said for many of our learned writers, philosophers, historians, scientists of international reputation, inventors, engineers, economists, and educators. So many of them are decadents, holding on to outmoded values of the past. Sometimes the more materialistically "liberal" and "progressive" and modern and up-to-date they fancy themselves to be, like their fellow Roman liberal and progressive decadents of two thousand years ago, the more reactionary blindlings time will prove them. These busybodies of materialistic liberalism, of mere economic internationalism, of socialistic distributivism, of political paternalism, of expedient pragmatism are a-work at everything except the main thing, getting man back to God. They are a-work with everything except the most important of all— the Love of God, basic principles of truth, basic morality. They should be a-work replacing the outmoded and outworn tests of value in the primacy of life, in objects and gadgets and wealth and security, in materialism and pragmatism, by the Love of God, preaching and demonstrating the Love of God. For the rare Sorokins, Sainte Thérèses, Bernadettes, Lucias, Péguys, Dostoievskis, Werfels, Dulles, Pacellis there are legions of John Deweys, Whiteheads, Russells, Perrys, Beneses, Streits, Lavals, Wilsons, Lenins, Roosevelts, Hitlers, Stalins, Maurois, Ehrenburgs, Steinbecks, Hemingways, Marshal Fields, intent on building ephemeral worlds in terms of the primacy of life, things, sensations, pleasures, earthly wealth, power, force, cartels, economic blocs, financial ententes, international federations, Teutonic, Latin, Anglo-Saxon blood brotherhoods, Slav alliances, all doomed to failure to the degree that they do not rest on Christ, all jetsam in the irresistible current of the future, a basic change away from one type of civilization to an entirely different one. The restoration of our world cannot be made on the little inadequate sensate reforms proposed by our "liberal" and "progressive" reactionaries; nor can it be made by a return to the "normalcy" which the conservatives cherish. This restoration cannot be made by a return to the past. A return to the past is vain, and impossible. It cannot be made by little, timid improvements. The entire world has to be rebuilt and its moral, social, intellectual and international order set in motion again under God and inspired with the Love of God. True civilization in our time can be obtained only by basing society upon Christ.

The spiritualist of 2800 with regard to our time, like the spiritualist of 800 with regard to Rome, will see that so many of our "leaders" and our headliners in practically every field have had no vital concept of the forces in motion with us, that our presidents and führers and writers and philosophers and educators were true decadents, the blind, selfish, deluded Neros and Vespasians and Caligulas and Senecas and Quintillians, all trying to pump life into institutions which are dying or dead, to give the mask of health and vigor where there was only disease and decay and corruption. He will see that the real leaders and creators of our time were those who insisted on the primacy of the things of God over the things of earth, on the spirit over the flesh, on absolute standards of morality and truth and justice and decency and mercy over expediency and pragmatism and operationalism and force and power, on the Love of God before all else. The choice is ours. Like St. Paul we can be fools with Christ before men, or we can be fools with men before God.

The folly of blindness

The first sentences of this book were a quotation from Christ flaying the blindness of a sensate world very much like our own. It came from His story of Lazarus and Dives. Dives, *i. e.* the rich man, was suffering in hell from his sins. He was not in hell solely because he was rich or solely because he had been a sensatist. He was in hell because, in ways which Jesus did not deem it necessary to tell us, he had violated the laws of God and probably also those of man. His wealth and luxury and sensatism doubtlessly facilitated his descent into perdition. They were not alone the causes of Dives' condemnation. Dives in his torment cries out to Lazarus, the former beggar at his gate, who is now in heaven, to go back and warn his brothers and his friends lest they also follow Dives' mode of life and come into his place of torment. Lazarus was not in heaven simply because he had been a beggar. Vagabondage *per se* is no virtue just for its own sake. He was in heaven because as a beggar he had been a virtuous man. Christ in this story is not trying to say that all beggars go to heaven or all Dives go to hell. He is flaying the blindness of the sensatists to any test of value except their own. For when Dives pleads with Abraham to send back Lazarus from the dead to warn his brothers, Christ makes one of the most forceful statements He ever made. He has Abraham say to Dives that if one should rise from the dead, should begin to prophesy among the sensatists of Dives' and his brother's type, even then they would not believe.

To those who know what is going on in our present century this statement of Christ's should be extremely interesting and it should ring very true. Yet, those who

have some inkling of the nature of our age should not be
arrogant or proud in their knowledge and foresight of the
significance of their time. They should know that their
knowledge is a gift of God like any other gift, that it is
a talent and should be put to work. They should be humble
in their knowledge, and at the same time share it with
others, preach the glad tidings that a new world is being
born. They may even have some dim knowledge of the
rôles, great or humble as they may be, which they can
play. Their insight may be no pure joy to them. It may
frequently be burdensome, even hard to bear. They share
the common difficulties of those who are *said* to be born
before their time. Yet, they are not really born before
their time. They are of it. They are transition figures.
The rôle of creativity is rarely easy. But neither should
they complain. They should be deeply grateful for the
insight and the grace God has granted them. For without
their knowledge the time would seem doubly dreadful,
doubly hard to bear, because it would be meaningless.
They should be humbly but deeply confident. There is not
one shred of doubt about the truth of which they have a
glimpse, not one shred of doubt about the end of the vision
of Dostoievski and Claudel and Péguy and the recent
Popes. They may be astonished that others do not see.
Their obligation is to try to make them see. The insight
that God has given them should not be held under a bushel
and the men who have a vista of the future are not holding it there. It is good news that a better world can be
built than any that has ever existed before and it should
be shouted from the housetops. The Father does not wish
that His wedding guests should be few. He wants all
men to share in His banquet. They need to be compelled
in from the highways and the by-ways and sometimes given

a strong push if they are unwilling.

Yet, the unwillingness of modern man to be a guest at the banquet of the Father in a world that God challenges us to build is admittedly nothing short of astounding. It is genuinely difficult to comprehend why so many men in our time are slow to grasp what is going on, that so many, seemingly of their own free volition, are wilfully blind to the world about them, to the world in the past of them, to the world in the future of them.

It is in this respect that the statement of Christ's is so interesting. It certainly throws light on the situation today. Verily if one should rise from the dead, he would not be believed. *Suppose* one should rise from the dead in the midst of our decadent sensate civilization of today and tell us what the future is! How would he be treated? He would be whisked away promptly to the nearest Freudian psychological or psychiatric laboratory so that the psychologists and the psychiatrists, these modern modish witch doctors of our mechanistic pagan jungles, these mumbo-jumboists of contemporary western voodooism, might go to work on him and pronounce him a subject sorely in need of their cares and cures and try to liberate him from his prophetic hallucinations and delusions. And if he were obdurate enough in his insistence on being risen, he would be carefully guarded by our modern blindlings in the best humane sociological fashion and insulated from the rest of society both for his own sake to save him from being ridiculed in an unbelieving world as well as to save the unbelieving world from such disturbing and annoying phenomena. Like Christ he would certainly be accused of stirring up the people. It would never occur to our modern stupidly complacent Westerners that perhaps the one thing they need above all else *is* to be stirred up about the developing rottenness and materialism and paganism and evil of our modern sensate world since the last Renaissance.

In a sense we have, however, not one man risen from the dead but a whole civilization risen from the dead to prophesy among us. We have the sensate world of Rome. The record of a sensate world very much like our own in its decay stands potentially accessible to all who would learn. Any good Latin major—if anyone any more majors in Latin—from the least decadent of our American colleges and universities should know, at least, something of our time. Perhaps it is to ask too much of our contemporary decadents to suggest that they major in Latin. It is also unfortunately quite possible that in the midst of ferreting out the meaning of words and the thumbing of dictionaries in a poorly taught Latin major they would never get at the spirit of the great books of Latin literature and history they would read; and it would, thus, be indeed difficult to say which was the greater dullard for missing so much, the student or the teacher. But, at least, to anyone who is really alive to the literature, the history, the thought, the philosophy of old Rome, the significance of our time should not pass unheeded. To those who have viewed with inspired awe the colossality of the shells and ruins of the Roman sensate world throughout Italy and so much of France and Africa and even in England and Germany, some insight should have come, were they not totally blind. And to all who read of or participate in the upheavals of our time—and that is well nigh all of us—there should come some inkling of the truth, were modern man not so wilfully and obdurately dull.

Yet, it is undeniable that Christ was right; that if one

should rise from the dead and begin to prophesy among this generation, it would not believe. It would not believe one risen or twenty risen or the whole world of Rome risen about it. Yet it *will* believe within fifty or a hundred or two hundred years. It will believe because the impact of events will force it to believe. If it by its free volition wills now to be blind, continues to will that way, prefers to will that way, then it will be forced to believe the hard way, the way of continued chaos and upheaval, of war and revolution, of sorrow and misery and wretchedness, until man accepts the challenge of His God and builds a right world to replace his wrong one.

Obviously those who speak out in our time for the world to come back to Christ do not wish to be considered as ones risen from the dead nor as ones speaking in terms of divine prophecy. In a vague way what they are awkwardly saying may in a sense be stumblingly and gropingly prophetic. Yet, their interpretation will be, at best, imperfect. It will contain much blundering and, perhaps, some genuine error. Living in a generation only ankle-deep in the future, in the New Renaissance of the Spirit, they as yet see things only darkly and in broad outline. What they gropingly sense, coming centuries will see face to face and in detail. What the men of our time who possess some slight insight into the future desire in a very special way is to have God's blessing so that they may say nothing which is contrary to His truth or the working of His will, that they will say nothing which will make the future one iota harder to be born, nothing that will lead others into even the slightest error. They desire rather, that they may help the future to be born, that they may express to their brothers the meaning of our time, that they may work in unison with the will and purpose of God.

To the psychologists and psychiatrists they reply and underline that they are not risen from the dead. If they claimed to be, the "modernists" and "liberals" would hold them quite mistaken and insist they are not really risen, that they are still quite dead, that they should do the decent thing and clamber back into the coffin and pull down the lid, and remain with the dead, where they belong. For the modern blindlings do not wish to be disturbed as they set about building their bright and happy new sensate world of security and wealth, of the materialist "internationalists'" paradise, of the Cairo and Teheran and Yalta and San Francisco and London and Paris and Moscow conferences, of the Anglo-Saxon-brotherhood, of the hegemony of "peace-loving" nations of the three or four or five "great" powers, of social and economic and political Utopias. God grant that the good seeds in these movements—and there are good seeds in them—may be sifted from the bushels of chaff in which they are buried so that our future can really be born with a minimum of travail.

Particularly, the men who understand something of our time, do not claim to be risen from the dead because to claim such would be a ridiculous lie and they try to speak the truth as simply and sincerely and as eloquently as they can, for they want to be believed and understood by as many as possible so as to help the new world under God into being. It is only in seeing and understanding our future, believing in it, ceasing to fear it, and, above all, in ceasing to cling to the dying, uncreative past, that man's free will will have the widest play in shaping the future and reducing to a minimum the chaos and disruption and upheaval which are to a certain extent inevitable in the course of the transition into future tests of value. Therefore, it is not only advisable but necessary that as large a number of people as possible understand what is going on in our time, so that they may help the future into being, participate in its creation, and use their free will as God intended—creatively, not as delaying, stultifying, disruptive reactionaries. If we will to create our future aright in our time, we can guide it well into its course. If we insist on clinging to the outmoded values of the past, the transition into the future will be a frightful one, forcing us by the sheer impact of physical reality, by the actual destruction of the world around us, away from the world of earthly things to which blindly we may cling, driving us by the combined effects of the calamities of War, Revolution, Famine, Pestilence, the dread Four Horsemen, away from our materialism and mechanism and decadence. This would be the *hard* way into our future. The wrong use of our free volition will simply make the future terribly hard, a veritable *dies irae,* an inferno of increasing horror. It will not alter an iota the general trend away from a decadent sensate world into a creative spiritual one. The right use of our free volition will, however, make for our salvation and will render easier the way for coming generations to use their free will for their salvation. It will go far toward assuring that the coming civilization of the spirit will be the very best epoch which Western man has known. This is the circle of choice within which God allows the free will of man to operate. No generation of men probably has ever had before such vast opportunities to will for good or evil as the men of our century. God has allowed us a most vast range. Those who have some inkling of this in our time must write and speak and humanly try to do their part to bring others to understand our age and to comprehend the rôle that they should play in it. Ours is the choice to use our free wills aright and we shall not be forgiven in this world, nor perhaps in the next, if we make a wrong choice in our time.

For our errors will be visited not only on us but on our children's children for many generations. If we make the right choices in our time by our own free will, the future will be a glorious one, a better one than any out of the past. If we do not, we may be sure that the next several centuries will be dreadful to contemplate. Our transition period will be more horrible than any of the transitions of the past. Modern science in its multiplication of the instruments of destruction, modern industry in its capacity to produce them, the speed of modern transportation to get such instruments of destruction rapidly from one area to another are enough to guarantee a much greater chaos than even that which prevailed in the disintegration of the last sensate culture, that of the Roman Empire. The whole world is now accessible to the upheaval. Almost no area can escape. Each succeeding upheaval can make the preceding one seem almost gentle; the trend of the future, if we make the wrong decisions, will be a mounting crescendo of misery and wretchedness. The broad nature of our time should be before the consciousness of men as soon and as widely and as constantly as possible. It is only in getting at least some approach to a synthetic grasp of the character of our age that it can be comprehended and met creatively.

We must understand clearly that we are living in a New Renaissance, the opposite in nature from the Renaissance of 1200-1600, similar in nature with regard to the tests of value which it will evolve and establish to the spiritual Renassance of the first four centuries A. D. The last Renaissance of seven hundred years ago was a rebirth of the world of things, of everyday reality, of science, of the senses, of materialism and mechanism and paganism, in short, of the non-Christian philosophy of the primacy of life. It was a rebirth of Rome and the values by which Rome lived. Our present Renaissance is a rebirth of the spirit, is a rebirth of the tests of value of the medieval world, is a rebirth of Christianity. Six hundred years from now, regardless whether the transition centuries are unbelievably violent and chaotic or relatively gentle, the entire western world will be living again by the values of eternity and absolute truth, of God and man's relation to Him. This period of transition is irrevocably in motion. The old sensate world has decayed beyond the possibility of recovery for, at least, another thousand years. It is a period of the rebirth of the new (the spiritual, the medieval, the absolute) and the death of the old (the sensate, the "modern", the relative). Man can no more halt this Renaissance than he can quiet a hurricane, arrest a volcano from erupting, or stay the quaking of the earth. Rome and modern times are giving away again to a civilization of the spirit.

We are living in the sunset of a declining Rome and modern world. We must not mistake the sunset glow for the real promise of the future, lest darkness engulf us before we know in what direction lies our dawn. This is our great danger. No transition period, no Renaissance ever stood in greater peril of failing to form its future aright. The blindness and self-complacency of ancient Rome on its threshold into the future were not as great as those of our modern world on the threshold of its future.

There is no cause for bleak, long-range pessimism such as that which imbues the great German philosopher,

Spengler, who believes that Western civilization is irremediably ruined and that all that remains for us moderns to do is to ride with the whirlwind, stoically and paganly accept the inevitable, and grasp as much glory and greatness out of our *Götterdämmerung* as we possibly can. Western civilization is too tough to be so easily ruined. Nor will the repeated wrong choices of succeeding generations permanently annihilate Western civilization. We have, at least, three thousand years of existence and we have survived apparent chaos before. Even if atomic bombs and lethal rays and radio active gases and fog should destroy or render uninhabitable every city and town in the Western world, some men would still survive, ideas and faith and God would still survive, some books and memories would still survive; there would be plenty of wherewithal to begin civilization anew, although such a new beginning admittedly would be terribly hard.

One may, however, agree with Spengler on the need for at least a healthy amount of pessimism now. The future does impend most menacingly. There are, however, hopeful signs. Spengler does not see them; and he has no grasp at all of the possibility of an alternative to our present decline. But even if the worst should come to pass, Western civilization will survive. That is, our future will be born in travail and blindness and chaos, if need be, that is, if we will wrongly; with understanding and creativity, if we will aright. But born it will be. Western civilization will not perish. In its best form Western civilization is Christianity, and God has guaranteed that the gates of Hell shall not prevail against His Church. As long as the Christian Church survives, Western civilization in its very best form survives. Western civilization survives even if it has to betake itself to the East to find the human stock in whom to inhabit—a fate not at all impossible not only through the blindness of modern war but also through the perhaps far more fatal suicide of birth control.

The great tragedy for us in the West will lie in the worst's coming to pass, that we misuse our free will so stupidly and wrongly as to bring generation after generation of chaos on ourselves, Spengler's long range pessimism is in this respect salutary. He realized, as few men have, the nature and seriousness of our time as a period of decadence. One of the principal sources of our danger is the fact that very few realize its seriousness or its import. The Second World War of our century, coming so soon after the terrible one of 1914-1918, should have been clear enough a source of warning to our world that it is decadent and needs to be born anew. It should also have given insight into the nature of the decadence and the remedies which must be taken. Instead, it has been to countless millions a force for obfuscation of the real issues involved and an encouragement to cling to false values. The Second World War and the "peace" which follows it gave rise to false hopes—already half dashed to pieces —and to a complacency that were not paralleled in Rome at the brink of its decline almost two thousand years ago. The optimism which has recently obtained concerning our immediate future is false, far more deleterious than Spengler's long range pessimism.

CHAPTER THREE

OUR MISPLACED FAITH

The passion for sensate satisfaction

IT WAS, PERHAPS, inevitable that the War should lead to
a facile optimism regarding sensate values. Modern war
is so harsh that men shrink from its realities. Then also
both sides use approximately similar propaganda techniques and promise a better sensate world after the war.
In the midst of horror they prop up the sagging morale
of their population by the hope of better things to come.
Thus, so many people on both sides have been led to believe that the termination of the war and victory would
bring them a "new order". The expression, "new order",
"new deal", has been an omni-present morale builder for
every nation. It has been universally employed. The Japa-
nese, the Germans, the Russians, the Poles, the Italians,
the English, the Dutch, the Belgians, the Greeks, the Slo-
vaks, the Finns, the Czechs, the Norwegians, the Chinese,
the Americans, the Australians, the Canadians, the French
have all been fighting for the "new order", and they have
been naturally led to assume it would be a better order.
Else why should they fight? Then too, the War in many
people has tended to foster a passion for easy sensate
values, no matter how lowly and transitory they might

be. There has been the usual eat-drink-and-be-merry-for-tomorrow-we-die form of sensate hedonism which always prevails in war time. There likewise has been the greed for booty and plunder, the easy acquisition of other peoples' property, which in war appeals to many elements who in times of peace would be held in check by the more rigid disciplines and laws of a tranquil order. Such elements have surged upward in their savage greed to get, to have, and to enjoy what would have been impossible for them to attain in their respective countries if they had had to work for it with the order and perseverance necessary in a peace time economy. In addition, the Second World War has increased the hunger for facile sensate satisfaction on the part of unusually large numbers of more normal industrious, thrifty men and women. It has rendered countless millions sensately starved. The vast areas over which actual land and air battles have raged saw millions deprived of the most elementary sensate necessities. Never in the history of the world were so many people hungry, cold, homeless, uprooted as there have been in the recent war, millions and millions of them in Italy, in Germany, in Russia, Japan, China, Poland, England, France, Belgium, Holland, *etc.*, yea, over much of the surface of the earth. Even those areas which were not visited by the physical destruction of war at the hearth side felt the pinch of war rationing and war scarcity. Even the neutrals knew the tightening belt of war conditions as the channels of free exchange of goods were transformed into channels almost exclusively used for the destruction and misery of man. The sensate irony of this has been inescapable. In the midst of a sensate culture the sensate tests of value have physically tended to disappear. Thus, millions in real or imagined sensate hunger have longed for an easy return to sensate satisfaction. They have complacently assumed that when peace came, their sensate hunger would be satisfied.

False adulation and its results

Probably the chief reason for the greater complacency of the modern sensate world on the brink of its decline in comparison with that of Rome on the brink of its decline is the implicit faith of modern man in his sensate science. This situation too has been aggravated by the war. To those who have such implicit faith in science it was science and its applications which won the war. In the midst of war and their sensate starvation, they thought of science as the force which would bring them countless new and interesting "revolutionary" things and instruments and gadgets and foods at the end of the war. Science and industry also tentatively promised this, albeit more cautiously than their advertisements and pronouncements were interpreted by their devotees. People had faith not only in the older pure and applied physical science. They had perhaps even greater faith in the somewhat newer social science. They believed that in political science lay the secret of banning war and building a universal and permanent peace. They had faith in the science of economics to solve the troublesome problems of scarcity and distribution, unemployment and security. In psychology and sociology they blindly saw the keys to all sorts of Utopias in which they fancied only ideal personalities would be developed and all the causes for strife and strain within the social order itself would be once and for all eradicated. People were sensately hungry, even starved; they believed what they wanted to believe, no matter how unreal or unattainable it might be. And they were subtly, directly or indirectly, encouraged to believe it by the propaganda which was issued for their consumption from their national governments. There was an unreasoning faith in an internationalism's being born almost without effort, in international courts and police, and economic and financial controls which would solve almost everything. It was subtly, or not so subtly, suggested that all the people would have to do was to follow trustingly their leaders and führers, give all faith and power to them, and they would bring about a wonderful new world.

The faith in the better world, in the "new order", grew apace with the faith in all forms of science and with the faith in the propaganda by which the populations in the various nations were spoonfed. A terrible complacency, therefore, arose which held that most of our problems either were already solved or would be within a few months or years or, at the most, a few decades. In fact, it was pictured as unpatriotic or, at least, "perfectionist" to believe otherwise. This was the worst possible atmosphere for our new Renaissance. It stultified many people who might otherwise have had some chance of being alert to their time. It perhaps affected the so-called educated classes worse than the "masses" of common people. For the so-called educated classes formed the dissemination belts for propaganda during the war. They helped manufacture some of the propaganda for mass consumption. More important still they passed government propaganda on down to the "masses". In pep talks, bond rallies, *Winterhilfsreden,* public forums, patriotic appeals they helped the "common man" digest his propaganda. And by dint of frenzied participation they came to believe it even more than he. The ordinary man preserved a certain minimum of the traditional sense of the ages. He never had seen a Utopian millennium, and he was slightly sceptical that one was being born. Particularly in the rural, peasant, and farmer class, among people close to the soil, and, thus, close to the tradition of centuries, there is always a conservative tendency of common sense afoot to combat the facile delusions into which the urban laboring and "educated" classes can intoxicate themselves by over much talking.

Yet, now that some of these same urbanite elements have seen that the international ententes and united-what-nots, far from guaranteeing peace and ushering in the bright new world, are simply sounding boards for national prejudices and national horse-trading and the promotion of national schemes, for balance of power and the admiration of one's own pragmatic interest polished up to pass for idealism, their reaction can be equally fatal in the opposite direction against building a new world under God. Some of them have chamoleoned from facile optimism into bleak despair and speak of the inevitability of a third and fourth and fifth world war—if by any chance the poor old quaking world can stand so many dread visitations of Mars. It is so common for weak-minded people to rush from one error into the exact opposite. Those who give way to despair do not stop to realize that nothing brought on by man is inevitable—until man brings it on—that modern man has within his power to avert any purely man made catastrophe if only he uses his talents, his genius, his free will properly. There is no more justification now for bleak despair than there was for facile optimism. Our future admittedly impends most menacingly. But the menace could rather easily be dissipated if only man would will and act aright. Those who flit from facile optimism to bleak despair should see that there are crumbs of truth

in both their attitudes, or else they stand convicted as
utter mad men. For surely their attitudes cannot be pure
error: pure error should make no converts outside of
Bedlam. There is really sober cause for boundless optimism in our world: there is also sober cause for great fear.
Modern man must make the decisions the results of which
will prove whether the optimism or the fear was more
correct. Nothing, however, is inevitable—until it happens.

There is nothing wrong with internationalism and ententes and united-what-nots, unless they are wrong internationalism, wrong ententes, wrong united-what-nots. God
knows that one of the matters most sorely needed in our
poor, old battered world is union of all possible men and
ideas and forces—for the things of God. But union and internationalism which are based on pragmatism, selfishness,
mere self-interest window-dressed as enlightened idealism,
balance of power, materialistic self-promotion are not the
stuff out of which a proper world can be built. Material
advantage cannot successfully or rightfully be put before
the rights of men and of God. A sound international order
can rest only on pillars which are just both before men
and before God. It dare not even concentrate on men and
ignore God, for it is not logical to observe the creature
and ignore the Creator.

Only blindlings could ever have believed that international organizations based on pragmatism and horse-
trading and mere self-interest, organizations where the
name of God could not be revered, could ever be the
foundations of peace. But now that the eyes of a few men
are being opened to the shallow hopelessness of such organizations, there is no cause for utter despair. International organizations are still very possibly the mills of
God which can help grind out a proper future—*if* they

are proper international organizations. Modern men who
have tried only bad and pragmatic and materialistic internationalism should not, therefore, conclude that all internationalism is wrong and trust blindly in the future to
only their own strength. We need terribly to use all the
tools we have for the future. Internationalism rightly
conceived and rightly used is one of them. But right internationalism is a very high ideal, for it stands succinctly for
the Brotherhood of all men, regardless of race or color
or nationality, under the Fatherhood of God. Instead
of turning their backs on internationalism, modern men
should realize that they themselves are largely at fault
for allowing a poor, pitiful, pale specter of pragmatic internationalism to be foisted upon them for the real thing.
Modern men are in no small way responsible for this
fiasco themselves.

Most areas of the West have representative and
elected government. The electorates have been able to
choose the representatives they wished. In the past the
electorates have voted for those out of whom they thought
they could materialistically *get* the most. They have been
selfish, interested only in personal advantage. It may become clear to them some day that their criteria have not
been adequate ones, that in their mania for getting they
have manoeuvred themselves into positions where they
will get many dreadful things which they had not antici-
pated. They may learn that even in voting one cannot be
selfish, that it is more blessed to give than to receive. The
wise electorates of the world must soon face that they
must seek first the Kingdom of God and His Justice if
they do not wish to inherit the whirlwind. When the electorates of most of the nations of the West wish internationalism under God and according to God's laws, they

can have the proper sort of representatives at the council tables of the world. Admittedly, not all nations have free electorates to choose such representatives. But the contagion of such an example is a disease civilization might well try to contract as an alternative to the despair and pessimism which now begin to brood like an incubus over certain quarters of the world. The Kingdom of God Christ has admirably compared to the leaven which does not rest until all is leavened. It is one of the most astounding facts about Christianity that if one puts it into practice, it is easier for our brother to put it into practice also. And, if we do not live according to God's laws, we make it that much more difficult for our brother to do so. We are in this sense literally our brother's keeper.

Yet, when we speak of the pessimism which begins to pervade certain quarters of the world, we must face that the vaster millions have still not shaken off the facile optimism into which they were lulled by the propaganda of the war. Particularly among the urban millions, but not exclusively among them, the war still has left an aftermath of implicit faith in the future and a complacency about it which are frightening. The overwhelming majority of Westerners are still blindly convinced that they are moving into a future just around the corner which is the exact opposite in its nature and tests of value of that into which they are *actually* moving. This blindness can certainly cause disaster and chaos which, if not on the Spenglerian or Wagnerian terms of a twilight of the gods, will be at least on a scale which makes one shudder to contemplate.

The faith of the modern world in all forms of science, physical and social, has become so unreasoning and implicit as to be one of the real forces for reaction in our time, one of the real forces to make the future chaotic. Inasmuch as a sensate world places its tests of value principally in things, in objects, in material possessions, the force which helps to satisfy its wants is the force to which the sensate world pays tribute. It is science particularly applied science, which makes possible most of the *things* by which a sensate world lives and takes its comfort and enjoyment. Science is a main contributor to the sensate happiness of a sensate society. For it is science which creates the sources of happiness, which makes its things. It is science which has given our modern world its electric refrigerators and to the Roman world its snow water coolers. It is science which built the great roads, the gigantic buildings, the vast colosseums and arenas, the swift chariots, the colossal engineering feats, and the formidable machines of war of ancient Rome. It is science which has built similar things for the modern world and mutiplied them a thousandfold over those which the last sensate society possessed. A sensate world is possible only so long as its science contributes preponderantly to the welfare and aggrandizement and happiness of a sensate population and to their increase and growth. When science begins to contribute powerfully also to the misery and wretchedness of sensate man and to his destruction and decrease, the sensate culture has passed its zenith and has begun to decay. This is one of the most inescapable facts of any sensate decadence and is so little understood in our time. Such contradictory dualism is one of the most inherent defects of a sensate culture. The very stuff out of which it builds its world is always also potentially the matrix in which is nurtured the destruction. The contradictory dualism of science is one of the most important sources of danger in our time, a force for almost infinite destruction

123

as well as one for almost infinite creativity.

We should, perhaps, not expect science to contribute exclusively to the welfare of sensate man. This it has never done and probably never will do. But if we judged by science alone—and we dare not, for it is just one of the many important aspects of our modern society—we should be correct in assigning the beginning of the decay of our sensate civilization to the second half of the nineteenth century[1]. During the second half of the nineteenth century the evolutionary theories of Darwin became popular. Darwin himself admittedly in many respects is scarcely to be blamed over much for the unfortunate results which his theories had upon the world. There is nothing in evolution, properly understood, inconsistent with Christian philosophy. It does not belittle God in any way to conceive of His planning foresight and creativity working through millennia. It might even help man gain a more adequate idea of the all embracing, creative Love of God for His creation. Nevertheless, through ramifications of thought which were, perhaps, inherent in the Darwinian postulates, mechanistic interpretations became prevalent in the West. Millions lost their Faith and their wisdom in the new secularism of mechanism. The world began to be dehumanized, a process bearing its logical fruit in the horrors of our own day, where man is frequently treated less sacredly than any machine, because he is cynically held to be less valuable than a machine. Through the influence of mechanistic theories of evolution, never scientifically proven, but for all that widely promulgated, man began to be stripped of his dignity, to be left a cringing, lustful animal, a physico-proton complex, worth in a laboratory way some insignificant sum of money; and particularly left prey to all the concomitant immoral and inhumane treatment which has been accorded man in the twentieth century—a treatment, however, quite logical in view of the soulless, mechanistic explanations of man current in the modern world.

Sensate science should ennoble man, add to his aggrandizement and self respect. The evolutionary doctrines robbed him of his nobility and uniqueness, ranked him with the "other" animals, and began the stress upon the animal nature of man, even his bestiality, a movement which has not by any means as yet begun to run its full course of decadence in many ramifications of science, art, literature, and philosophy. Hard upon the heels of the Darwinian theories came those of Wundt and Freud with the result that man was scarcely even left as a whole animal but was rather a part of one, composed largely of glands, a hopeless complexity of libidos, urges, and frustrations, a cringing, lustful, unlovely mechanism. It was also during the second half of the nineteenth century that science began to make accessible a vast corpus of knowledge and instruments which could be used indifferently for the welfare or injury of man. Sensate science *per se* is indifferent to moral and human values. It is neither good nor bad. Its implementation toward good or evil is entirely supplied by man. In the great founders and establishers of modern sensate science, in Galileo, Copernicus, Bacon, Descartes, Newton, Leibnitz, Harvey, Fabricius, Leeuwenhoek, Priestley, the creativity of the sensate period was in the ascendancy and their work redounded to the sensate good of man. In the nineteenth century the curve of creativity was rounding off at its maximum, had, as the mathematicians say, reached its critical point, and the forces which in earlier centuries would have worked more readily to the sensate good of man became less creative and could turn indifferently to bring forth sensate good or sensate evil. Science came to be loaded with great powers for destruction as well as for creation. It began to work against sensate man as well as for him.

Science, of course, still contributes to the sensate happiness of man and doubtless will continue to do so for a rather indeterminate period, perhaps centuries or more. Moreover, if we get into our future properly, there are almost no limits to the extent to which it should contribute to the welfare of man. But it has begun also to contribute mightily to his unhappiness and misery and degradation and to his decrease. It is science which makes the bombs, the planes, the tanks, the guns, the poisonous gases, the weapons of war as well as penicillin and sulpha drugs and beautiful yachts. The aeroplane is indifferent to an errand of mercy or of destruction, whether it drops the gospel of Christ or atomic bombs. The radio can emit with equal effortlessness a tirade of hate and lies and infamy or the preachment of God's Kingdom. The same science which gives the aeroplane and the radio also gives the bomb which can blast them and their owner into maimed, twisted, unrecognizable masses of themselves, sear them and burn them into disintegration. The same science which helps to cure the diseases and maladies of man and saves thousands of human lives gives also the instruments of birth control by which man decreases the growth of his race just as it gave similar instruments of birth control to ancient Rome. It can snuff out before conception and keep from any life at all potential millions of human beings for the thousands it maintains a few years longer once they are born. Our world and Rome in the midst of sensate marvels have often become so decadent as to have lost the will to create in proper numbers others to enjoy the sensate happiness of which we claim to be so proud.

Many unconsciously sense that our sensate world is slipping, non-creative, insecure. If moderns really had any faith in the validity of the values to which they cling, they would have more courage and realize that the gift of life to others is the greatest power which lies within them to bestow.

Science, therefore, at the present time is contributing both to the happiness of man and his misery, to his curing and his destruction, to his aggrandizement and to his degradation. By the very nature of the dualistic contradiction which is taking place in science, the main prop and stay of a sensate world, the real producer of the things by which a sensate world lives, our modern sensate world is yielding once more to the spiritual just as ancient Rome did.

Such contradictory dualism in science was inevitable. Science can never lead to really basic enough truth to be a permanent prop for the tests of value of a civilization. Its method is analytic, it tears apart, subjects to examination, investigation, and analysis. It studies more and more about less and less, investigates smaller and smaller segments of reality with greater and greater scrutiny. Truth, however, is a whole, is synthetic. It is not divisible and fragmentary. It cannot be isolated into departmental segments and its parts neatly filed away into separative pigeon-holes without destroying the unity which is its very essence. The only way to get at truth is by synthesis, and the complete synthesis is God. The modern sensate scientific method leads in the direction away from truth, not toward it. It leads to specific facts. That is, most modern science leads, in whole or in part, to isolated and detached fragments of impotent reality. By its analytic and fragmentary method it leads away from the synthesis of truth.

What moves away from truth leads *toward* error, and, if it moves enough, it eventually moves into error. Modern analytic science is by its very nature error-bound and not infrequently it has arrived at actual error. Modern science has so isolated itself from complete truth as to have lost its vision and perspective and it has sometimes become so blinded as no longer even to know in which direction truth lies. Even in dealing with things, the area in which science usually feels itself quite adequate, it cannot deal with their most important nature, their *essence*. It can treat not of their being but only of their qualities, their *accidents*. It can treat only of the characteristics and properties of things, not of their being, their essence, the reality of the things themselves. It can, for example, describe an apple, weigh it, break it into its constituent elements, measure its malic acid content. By its processes of selectivity it can improve its flavor, the color, the texture, the size. It can hasten its maturity and lengthen the time during which it will cling to its tree. But it cannot treat of its essence, the "appleness" of an apple. When it tries to, it becomes pitiful and immediately shows its limitations by speaking of its characteristics. With all its fragmentary facts about an apple, it really does not know what an apple *is* or why it is. It can treat about apples. But it misses the most important existence of an apple, its essence, that which makes it uniquely and exclusively an apple.

This is not to deny in any way that analytic and applied science in the past centuries has yielded a solid body of objective truth and reality which any culture would disregard to its harm. To ignore the experiments of Pasteur or the reality of the airplane would be potentially suicidal and foolish. But it is to say that on the results and facts of science must be imposed an order from without—an order greater than science. Totalitarianism has already done this the wrong way by subjecting and enslaving science to the state. In any proper order, however, the order imposed on science should be in harmony with divine law. It should be imposed so as to make science work in harmony with God. Science itself is amoral, capable of being turned either to good or bad ends. The order imposed on science from without should be in terms of the honor and service and Love of God. The airplane and pasteurization under God, helping to create God's Kingdom, are all very proper and real and beneficial. If we lose them, we lose a great deal. But they are not primary. Science is not the independent, self-sufficient creature much of modernity has naïvely imagined it to be. It is itself only a part of creation and often only a very humble impotent part with no primacy in itself. Modernity in paying prime attention and even almost worship to science has been giving its service at false and pagan altars.

Modern science in its self sufficiency and pride is not infrequently apostate from truth. It is always strictly and terribly limited as all honest scientists are beginning slowly to admit. But scientists have not always been so humble or so honest. At the turn of the twentieth century there was not a rare tendency in science and among scientists to believe that there was no realm which could escape their probing. They would investigate everything and eventually come to know everything. The popular lecturers and charlatans of science unfortunately spread this ill-placed confidence among the masses of people who came to have an innocent and child-like faith in science which science never deserved and which in its new-found humility it sincerely deplores. Science in many important respects is already beginning to make its transition into a civilization of the spirit in keeping with our New Renaissance and our changing tests of value. It already knows it has no keys to the really basic problems of our time which are all moral and metaphysical ones, not scientific ones. It also knows that it can be a force toward good or evil as men prefer to use it, that the very use, and beyond that, the existence of science, are moral problems. But the popular mass faith in science, in spite of the dawning humility of honest scientists, remains well-nigh unshaken. This popular faith is one of the most important constituents of the self-complacency of our decaying sensate world in regard to its future, one of the principal causes for the prevailing blindness which fails to comprehend the nature of our time. This blindness really goes further than the failure to comprehend. It thoroughly misunderstands and views as inevitable what will prove impossible. The blind and dull think that they are just around the corner from a quite wonderful and peaceful sensate world. Moving really into one type of world they fancy themselves to be moving into a quite different type. The convulsions and chaos which will result when the impact of physical reality comes to open the eyes of even the most dull may be, thus, of almost Spenglerian proportions.

The common denominator of dullardry

This condition of dullardry and inertia and blindness is the most alarming aspect of our time. It is precisely this condition which has contributed most of all to rendering the three previous, historically well known, transition periods in Western civilization from sensate culture to spiritual or from spiritual to sensate such convulsive, chaotic, volcanic, uncomfortable epochs. It is, therefore, quite logical to expect, but alarming to contemplate, that this time the unparalleled, almost universal, obfuscation as to the nature of our time will make our transition period a superlative of hellishness as it has already begun to be and gives convincing promise of continuing to be.

The blind in Greece of the third and fourth centuries B. C. did not know that the old spiritual culture was yielding to a sensate world of the new Hellenistic period, a sensate culture which was to be caught up from decadent Greece and passed on to its flourishing in Rome. As late as well into the fourth century we find the savage satire in the plays of Aristophanes against the decaying world, the crackling thunder in the oratory of Demosthenes warning of the future at the very doorstep, addressed to a world dull and uncomprehending of its time. With the blind and reactionary holding back the future the transition had to be made the hard way, the way of chaos and upheaval, war and famine and revolution and pestilence. Calamity, misery, and wretchedness brought on the future in spite of the dullards of Athens and Corinth and Thebes. Thus, it was the period of the Persian and Peloponnesian wars, of friction between the city states, of class and party strife, of starvation and pestilence. Thucydides, the great Greek chronicler of the transition period, sounds as modern as a diary from contemporary Europe.

Nor did the dull in Rome of the first centuries A. D. realize that their sensate world was in decay, even on the point of disintegration. The transition years of Rome into the future were sad years marked by the steady disintegration of one of history's greatest empires, by civil war and class strife from the time of the Gracchi onward, by the progressive impoverishment of a nation which was until the nations of the modern world unequalled in its riches, by the greedy upsurging of all materialistic elements, from proletarian and vagabond to bourgeois and patrician, "governed" by a dizzying, swift-passing array of general-emperors, by the inevitable socialization of the nation giving more *panem et circenses* to the mobs until almost everyone had almost nothing and a few had everything worth having, and, finally, by the recurrent attacks and successful invasions of the Gothonic hordes who broke into the Roman world hoping to share in the sensate wonders of which they had heard even in their far-away Teutonic homelands. The result of the transition was that Rome simply went to pieces like an over-ripe fungus. The path was broken into the spiritual future the hard way: the sensate values to which Rome had clung were clutched by the dullards until physical calamity simply dissolved them. But in spite of the Roman dullards the future was born.

The medievalists of the last Renaissance were likewise blind to their time, blind that a new world was being born in their very midst. Even cardinals and popes fostered and nourished in the transition centuries the very forces of sensatism in art and literature and science which were to buttress a new universal trend in the thought of the West and eventually to overthrow the spiritual world of the Middle Ages, disrupt and divide Christianity, and hurl wide open the flood gates to the onrush of the future. When only too late the medievalists realized the threat of the arising pagan future and tried impotently to arrest it, it was already engulfing them. As early as the middle of the fourteenth century Petrarch, the friend and secretary of popes and cardinals, in his *Secretum* said:

"I do not ask to be God and to possess eternity and to fill heaven and earth. I am a mortal and desire only mortal things. . . . It may be only glory that we seek here as long as we remain here, but that is right. Among mortals the care of things mortal should come first."

Two hundred fifty years later these were again fairly universally the standards by which vast multitudes of people were living for the first time in a thousand years. The transition itself was terrible. The creativity of Raphael, of Michelangelo, of Leonardo, of Rabelais and Petrach and Boccaccio and Villon did little to relieve the stark horror of the time for their contemporaries. War and revolution, famine and pestilence, the four horsemen of calamity, rode widespread over the face of Europe. The Black Plague scenes in Boccaccio's Italy of the 1340's could easily, *mutatis mutandis,* be torn from the record of the famine-war-disease ridden 1940's. But the future was born even if the medievalists were blind to it. The modern sensate pagan world triumphed in spite of them who did not know of its existence. Thus, transition follows transition. Spiritual yields to sensate and sensate to spiritual. Only the blindings remain constant, unseeing, uncomprehending, unyielding, holding back the future, rendering its travail needlessly prolonged and infernal.

In our present Renaissance the blindlings have unparalleled opportunities for making the transition hellish in a manner undreamed of before. They have already gone far toward making the twentieth century a true chaos of transition. The century is only half-ended. What they can and perhaps will accomplish in the second half of our century and onward for another century or so makes understandable the pessimism of Spengler even if one does not agree with it. Our blindlings will not really destroy Western civilization as Spengler fears. The future which will save it will be born in spite of them. They will not prevent the spiritual world of the future. But they can temporarily halt it and make the transition into it an almost unrelieved inferno. At the worst, by 2500 A. D the chaos of transition should be over. Our change will have been completed and the values of the spirit will again be the values by which men live. But in the years in between the young may die early and the survivors of wretchedness grow hastily and mournfully old.

It always lies within the power of transition centuries to understand their time and change their tests of value before being forced and shocked into new values by the rude fist of calamity. It has been, however, a fairly consistent record of the past that the more decadent values became, the more savagely men clung to them. If men voluntarily misuse their free wills and prefer to be blind in spite of the manifold indications of the trend of the future which are present if men would only open their eyes and *will* to see, they have only themselves to blame for the chaos they bring upon themselves. In the past transitions they have preferred to remain dull and uncomprehending. This time seems an exception only by the increased potentialities for the intensity of frightfulness. For this time the dull are communicating with one another on a scale impossible before. They can now plan more vast than ever their decadent sensate world schemes,— or think they can,—until the whole structure comes tumbling down about us all. The dull can now meet from the four corners of the earth and devise in a week what before could not have been dreamed of in years. The marvels of rapidity in communication which the decadent sensatists prize so much can prove equally instruments of perdition on a scale never before seen.

If the modern sensate world does not admit its decadence and open its eyes to our needfully changing tests of value, if it holds on to its outmoded sensate values wilfully and stupidly for the next several generations, our

134

time will be marked by repeated occurrences of war, of calamity, of hunger, pestilence, misery, homelessness, forced migrations, *déracinement* as it has begun to be. If the decadent sensate West in the future continues to hold to the primacy of the things of earth, what we see of misery and uncertainty about us in the world today is but a small part of the chaos and wretchedness and groping uncertainty we shall see in the time to come. Man will either give up his materialism and pragmatism by his own free will or he will be *forced* to do it over the future centuries by the shock of physical reality. If he holds on to his automobiles, his radios, his buildings, his hot-dogs and hot dates, his things, his comforts, his multidinous sensate objects and pleasures as prime tests of value, he will in the coming years see these things simply disappear into nothingness from the impact of bombs and disease and poverty and boundless misery. World calamity will follow upon calamity, until calamity seems to be the common denominator of existence. If man comes to realize the present decadence of his sensate world, of his science, his education, his philosophy, his morals, of his entire hierarchy of values and willingly discards them for the spiritual tests of value of the future, the transition can be relatively easy and certainly much shorter, much less chaotic and horrible.

The inertia of unwillingness to change is so pointless and useless. The future challenges us with a hope so much greater than any civilization of the past has ever offered. It is not only blind, it is really criminal of man not better to implement the great graces which God offers him. To exchange our poor inadequate world of things, of rivalries and competitions and hates and wars, a world all topsy-turvy with its quest and passion for the gifts of God, to exchange such a world for a world of the Love of God, of Love for the Giver of all gifts, a world of cooperation, of the brotherhood of man under God, a world seeking first His justice with His guarantee of abundant gifts beyond the present ability of man to produce, hamstrung as he is by his materialism and its resultant rivalries and hates and misspent energies, a world that challenges the dreams of man, a world that challenges his soul to un-vistaed soarings and uplifts to its Creator, appears so attractive that no sane man seemingly would be unwilling to give it a try, do all in his power to bring it as soon as possible into being.

Yet, we must face honestly that such is not the case, that the inertia of reaction, unwillingness to change, incomprehension of the nature of our age, are as yet the dominant notes of the twentieth century. We probably need to be immediately pessimistic, but with long range optimism, about the transition away from the sensate world. The blindlings will probably remain in control during this transition period as they already have done in those of the past. Such a fate for us, however, is doubly, stupidly unnecessary since in the dissolution of the last sensate world, that of Rome, we have a clear record of warning for our time if we were not too blind to read it. We could learn much about the dangers of our time by studying the books, the personalities, the ideas, the currents and trends of the Roman world almost two thousand years ago. If we knew well Roman history and literature and philosophy and thought, we should understand much more readily our own time. We should also be much more able to unmask our blindlings, comprehend them for what they are, a greedy, selfish, materialistic, pragmatic, expedient, dull pack, like uncomprehending parrots mouthing the ideas and platitudes of the past, ideas once creative, but which are now weak and flabby. Like the Roman dullards of twenty centuries ago our modern dullards seek their own aggrandizement and power and prestige, they follow their Lilliputian sensate goals and ambitions, they attempt to crush out the creative persons and forces that are a-work for the future, they try to cloak their ruthlessness under the shibboleths of the "common welfare" and "national expediency", the *Gemeinnutz*. Almost two thousand years ago the blindling Jewish high priest Caiaphas engineered the crucifixion of his Messiah by this same shibboleth, the common good: "One man should die for the people that the whole nation perish not." (John, XI, 50). Christ, the leader of the last Renaissance of the Spirit, well understood the blindlings of His day in a time so similar to our own. He called the blindlings of the last decaying sensate world by harsher names even than that of blindlings. He called them hypocrites, a generation of snakes and vipers, a shameful, blind deluded herd, of whom few indeed might hope for salvation.[2] He flayed them mercilessly day after day for the three years of His ministry and teaching until they finally succeeded in doing away with Him. But the dullards remained in control until the whole world of sensate Rome simply disintegrated. It may be much the same with us. Under such circumstances we shall deserve to be called the century of the misled. It is, in fact, already, clear that very many of the men in leadership in the various nations of our time are in places of leadership only because they are the supreme and dullard activist decadents leading their less active fellow decadents. Our "leaders" are so frequently leaders only of the dull and misled by whom they are elected and whom in turn they lead, or mislead, around by the nose. Such leaders are playing only a negative rôle for the future. They will only increase our misery. Our modern dullards will try as they did in ancient Rome to bolster up the declining sensate world by a vast array of impotent tricks of applied science, of economics, of sociology, and psychology. It sounds, for example, quite modern to read that in the days of Emperor Diocletian the Roman government tried to shore up the sagging girders of the sensate civilization by taking over control of business, fixing wages and prices, and determining the value of money. Valentinian III introduced the "modern" invention of the sales tax. A century earlier Valentinian I tried to convince the poor and wretched dispossessed classes of Rome that something was being done for them as he introduced socialized medicine by providing a physician for the poor in each of the fourteen districts of Rome. Such psychological, sociological, and economic tricks impressed many for a time, even the ancient psychologists, sociologists, and economists who invented them, but they staved off collapse only temporarily and actually prolonged the agony of transition into the new world.

For if Rome had gotten into the Christian spiritual world of the Middle Ages sooner and by less chaotic ways, it could have taken over its very excellent ideas of helping the poor by medicine and social legislation, taken over its knowledge and gifts of God. These, in turn, could have so readily found in the Christian Gospel an ideal background against which they could have been implemented into the greatest good for society. For certainly the Healer and Lover of the poor, the Source of all gifts, gave a most excellent model after Whom the

very considerable knowledge and wealth of Rome could
have been patterned into use. Instead, however, Rome
was so shattered that almost all its wealth and knowledge were lost, and the spiritual future wrongly deprived of what by special right should have belonged
to it, since it could have used the gifts of Rome to such
excellent purpose. Rome progressively impoverished and
ruined itself by its inertia of sensate reactionarism and
robbed and cheated the future most wrongfully, a future
which had very much better standards and principles
against which to use the treasures and wealth and knowledge than Rome ever had. But Rome went its own
blindling way, a world of the blind led by the blinder.
Heavy taxation and special privilege for the party bureaucrats sapped the vitality of the once prosperous sensate Empire. Many groups came to believe that they had
a right to live from the state without doing anything in
return. Taxation rose to preposterous levels to pay the
hordes of officials and to amuse and feed the idle, non-
producing city population. Bureaucratic control came to
rule private lives. As polybius had foreseen three hundred
years before, the whole decadent system boasted of its
liberty and democracy and progress and new ways. Birth
control flourished and if the newest devices and prepa-
rations for limitation of mankind failed, there was
always an abortionist around the corner to commit murder on the unborn for a small fee. Yet in the midst of
the decadency and the tricks of the dullards there was
the growing power of spiritual ideas, the rising Church
of Christianity.

The course of our sensate decline

The psychological, sociological, economic, technological tricks of the so-called liberals of today are often the real reactionary, backward forces of our time as they were in the Rome of nineteen hundred years ago. Such "liberals" will try to save decadent sensate values by socialism, by economic distributivism, by international controls, financial, political, military, and economic. At first, they will doubtless succeed in giving the sensate world more and more of what is worth intrinsically less and less. They will give it socialized standardization, mass production of things which are *sensately* inferior, less creative, less aesthetic. The sensate decline already in full course will be accelerated tremendously as sensate taste recedes, as quality yields to quantity, as the mass compulsion of socialism triumphs over sensate individualism. The better sensatists who will vainly *and* paganly struggle to defend an aristocracy of sensate values will be engulfed in the rising tide of mediocrity and eventually of inferiority. Compulsion will achieve mediocrity, surfeit will effect the inferiority. Symbolically, and perhaps actually, everyone will have for a time soy beans and soy beans and soy beans. They will eat them, build out of them, dress in them, and perhaps even ride or fly in them. And afterwards will come the deluge.

Education, after science one of the great sources of the pride of the modern sensate culture, will become poorer and poorer, more and more decadent, more and more "practical", devoted increasingly to the ephemeral and the expedient, so that almost everybody will know almost nothing. We have already made great "progress" in this direction; and the dullards in the various departments in many of our school and colleges and universities throughout the world are working twenty-five hours out of every twenty-four to accelerate our plunge into stupidity and ruin. The sensate education in its best creative period was built upon the humanistic outlook of Petrarch and his successors. Such humanistic education was unquestionably the best sensate education Western man has ever possessed, although it lacked from the beginning the abiding truth and deo-centricity of medieval spiritual education. Where Christian medieval education had stressed the love and knowledge and service of God and aimed at forming habits and attitudes in the young which would assist the recipients of education to love and know and serve God on earth so as to be happy with Him in eternity, the sensate humanistic education evolved in the last Renaissance was interested in making the recipients of education live as richly as possible among men and attain the terrestrial glory and promise which was held out to each according to his talents. It was man-centered rather than God-centered. It paid, indeed, a certain amount of lip service and, perhaps, a minimum amount of real service to spiritual values, since it was fundamentally sound enough to realize that a life with no spiritual values is arid and not conducive to the richest possible living. At the same time it was from the beginning sensate enough to keep the spiritual values at a plane where they did not interfere too obtrusively with this more serious business of rich living. Within these very serious sensate limitations, its concern with "the best which has been thought and written", its attention to the great books of human genius, its demands upon the perseverance and discipline and self-control of the individual, its challenge to develop the sensate best in man by acquainting him with the sensate best, its generally creative and elevating character are even now in the sad days of its decadence stimulating evidence of the excelence of humanistic education.

It, unfortunately, like all the rest of the sensate movement, bore within itself the seeds of its own destruction as the scholastic educators and theologians of the dying spiritual world of the Middle Ages knew from the very origin of humanistic education. Occupied with the *litterae humaniores* it too exclusively placed its stress on things human. Man instead of God was the center of interest in humanistic education. It became progressively more and more occupied with the immediate and utilitarian concerns of man. The chief exception to its exclusively man-centered curriculum developed fully two centuries after the Renaissance had firmly fixed such a trend; namely, as the Protestant Revolt tried to ingraft on the essentially non-religious character of the new sensate education certain compromise appendages which would facilitate the education of its clergy side by side with the education of the members of the sensate society destined to play purely secular rôles. This was a compromise which never seriously threatened the man-centered nature of humanistic education, largely because of the sensate compromise inherent in Protestantism itself. Begun as a literary gospel alive with the knowledge and books of man of the ancient world, humanistic education developed into a sensate gospel of the primacy of life. The *litterae humaniores* grew into a doctrine of the perfectibility of humanity itself as the supreme end and highest good. First stressing man and the better aspects of the earth-earthy, it eventually and quite understandably became increasingly concerned with immediacy as the vision of sensate man became narrowed and his creativity slackened. Now in full decay the descendant of humanistic education has split broadly into two savagely hostile camps.

The smaller one, that of the genuine, historical humanists, tries to preserve the broader outlook and the concern
for the sensate supreme good of man, his richest possible
living. They cling to the tradition of the sensate best and
with varying degrees of success barely manage to keep
alive the spark of humanism from complete extinction.
Sometimes they do no better than rattle the dry bones
of a bygone era, thinking that by their moving them they
really impart life to the humanistic skeleton. Blind, and
perhaps happily so, to the decadent trends of their time
they look backward to the restoration of a world which
is gone permanently for them and for many generations
to come. They are the sad but brave figures of every transition period holding on to the better creative values of
the past. In the midst of decadence they staunchly and
admirably refuse to become decadents. Among beasts they
refuse to howl with the wolves, and go through the
motions of acting like noble men. Many of them are men
of boundless courage and idealistic vision. Others are just
ordinary dullards who were helped by the innate excellence
of humanism in spite of themselves and unconsciously sense
that it is the best force which they have found in the midst
of decadence and hence defend it valiantly. They are playing a rôle similar to that which the virtuous and pious
religious played during the last Renaissance; although
surrounded by laxing standards and increasing amorality
of the arising sensate world most of the monks and nuns
and cardinals and popes and laymen clung to the spiritual
values of the past and flung the torch of spirituality on
to future generations who, in spite of hostile tempests,
have kept it always from quite flickering away, so that it
may be passed onward again to coming ages now the flame
of spirituality once more begins to burn high. The struggle

of our humanists is hopeless for a thousand years. But that will not deter their stout hearts from the battle. It may be that, if, unfortunately, the world of spirituality should ever yield again to the world of the sensate, the torch of humanism that they have protected bravely from complete extinction may once more flame again. Then over a long range period these better reactionaries of their time will not have played an entirely non-creative rôle.

The other educational camp of the modern humanists is much more numerous and in its extremes reaches almost abysmal depths of decadency. It appeals to all those inferior and genuinely decadent elements in a sensate society incapable of profiting by the excellence of a better humanistic education and who in their inferiority or laziness sense that it is beyond them and, therefore, rear up to destroy it, spitefully and savagely, as symbolic of their own inadequacy. Their movement, suggested ineffectively by Montaigne, was founded by the complete and savage "liberal" anarchist, Rousseau. Bloated by all the self-complacent mediocrities and inanities of thought from the atmosphere of the French Revolution, it triumphed during the nineteenth century and cannot be effectively challenged by sensate alternatives in the twentieth. It offers truly decadent sensate education for the decadents and makes everyone feel at home in its educational atmosphere, no matter how uneducable or lazy he may be. It concerns itself with lower pragmatic and expedient forms. It works under such slogans as education for everyday living, for a job, learn and earn. It is increasingly concerned with the practical, the contemporary, the vocational, and the ephemeral. Humanistic education was quite correctly, from sensate standards, concerned almost exclusively with the needs of man. But its decadent branch holds that such needs may be largely summarized under bread alone. It has ceased to be education at all and has become mere training. The decadent sensate educational system has become first and foremost a set of training schools devoted to useful knowledge and the crafts. Its chief business is to prepare successful business men, craftsmen, engineers, technicians, lawyers, doctors, preachers, barbers, bakers, welders, salesmen, mechanics, war-or-peace-time gardeners. Mastery is sought in such "arts" as amassing a fortune, farming, cooking, teaching, preaching, and bottle-capping. Elementary, secondary, higher education are all orientated in a narrowly utilitarian direction, paying scant attention, if any, to the forgotten purpose and values of truly creative sensate education, the richest possible living. Since most of the ideas and subjects of the older excellent humanistic education which make for "the richest possible living" are considered devoid of any immediate utility, they are scarcely given even lip service and play little part in the schools of the decadent sensate educational system in any of the major nations of the West. Instead, such education attempts to fit its sails into whatever direction the winds of the moment are veering. It tries to prepare its recipient for an immediate job and keep him off the public relief rolls for the several years the job may be in existence. Since the practical and the contemporary may shift almost from month to month, it remains permanently in a dither of upheaval and change. What it says today it belies tomorrow and contradicts the next day. It is marked by a constant turmoil of new subjects, new stresses, new techniques.

Like all decadent movements it stresses the importance of techniques. Forgetting that in the hands of genius or even of adequate normalcy any technique by grace of God may be creative, it believes that by attention to techniques it can force a creativity which is lacking in the very spirit of the times. By grace of God in the hands of the proper person any technique may be good. Lacking the spark of creativity a dullard with any technique, no matter how adequately or painstakingly it is taught, remains dull.

Modern decadent education has diluted the curriculum to a point either of ridiculous painlessness or utilitarian immediacy and utter materialism. It has largely lost the concept of quality and is concerned almost exclusively with quantity and mass. Worse yet, it assumes that time spent and "credit" earned are the earmarks of education. Because more people are in school longer, it blindly and woefully believes in its dull decadence that they know more. Attendance at modern educational institutions is viewed somewhat as an equivalent to time spent in penal houses of correction. One "does" his time and is then let loose upon society. In fact, a good penal institution may do more to uplift its inmates than an average educational institution does for its pupils. The immediate and practical utilitarian emphasis of decadent sensate education has lost all the wisdom and breadth of vision which was once inherent in humanistic education. A university in Germany under Nazism would give the same "credit" for a course in chemical warfare or applied agriculture as it would for one in the works of Plato. In fact, for the "good of the German people in its hour of trial before the throne of destiny" it would definitely foster the former and omit or even assail the latter. In any American college or university the *Iliad* of Homer or the works of St. Thomas are equated with a course in economics, sociology, or

speech-making. The decadents and mediocrities flock to
the latter because they feel at home with their fellow
blindlings. A report on the sex crimes of a tenement area
or a speech on "why I prefer skating to skiing" has a
hundred eager hearers while the works of Homer or of
St. Thomas lie almost neglected. No college would be
without its multiplication of courses in economics, sociology
or speech, years upon years of them; only the very best
would offer a single full year in the works of Homer or
St. Augustine, and then only "when the demand for the
course is sufficient to 'justify' its being offered." Little but
the most commonplace and ordinary and utilitarian is ever
studied in the modern decadent sensate education; the
content is the expansion of the obvious and the practical
and the utilitarian upon the part of the dull for the benefit of the duller. St. Thomas and Homer might make
demands upon modern sensatists and make them uncomfortably sense their inadequacy. But even economics, sociology, and speech are only the *academic* cellar in America.
If one goes into the *vocational* or the "practical" field, the
findings are almost unbelievable. Tap-dancing, applied cos-
metics, elementary swimming, intermediate swimming, advanced swimming, advanced bun-making, and forty-four
courses in lumbering in one university are equated in
"credit" (and undoubtedly surpassed by number of en-
rolees) with the New Testament or the works of Dante.

The blindling workers in the field of education have
lost all vision of whence they came and whither they are
going; preoccupied with immediacy and minutiae they
plunge madly into stupidity and ruin, dragging with them
the youth entrusted to their care. Professors of rank and
authority in American or foreign universities boast of
never having read a great book. They would hold that it

is not immediately practical and has nothing to do with the forty-four courses in lumbering. Many of them are totally uneducated themselves and actually cannot read except in the most limited legalistic sense of the term. They cannot read and do not, or do not and cannot. The better students in our contemporary educational institutions sense the decadency ofttimes better than their professors and usually do little or no work at all. Such students, born between the two worlds, by their very nature refuse to belong to the decadency of the present and are not yet alert enough to catch the trend of the future. The honors and the Phi Beta Kappa keys go to the dullard souls not yet alive to the decadency of the times who have acquired the habit of patience and routine amid the minutiae and trivia of contemporary education. (*Peccavi, Agnovi, Confiteor.*) With the possible exceptions of the fields of contemporary politics, international relations, literature, and morals, in no area of the modern sensate culture is our decadence so devastating and so depressing as it is in the field of education. As soon as the humanities decline, it is evident that the sensate educational world comes a-tumbling with them.

However, the socialistic and technological and liberal and educational contortions of our time will fail as they did in ancient Rome. Socialism and liberalism which begin by everybody's having more and more of less and less value will finally end, as it did in Rome, by almost everyone's being reduced to universal poverty and ignorance and misery, by almost everyone's having nothing and a few bureaucrats or party members having everything. One of the most fatally dangerous groups of reactionary blindlings of our time are all those sincere but obfuscated, provincial, and ignorant materialistic "liberals" and secularists who are blind in thinking that they can prop up a decaying world and arrest its decadence. They actually hold back the future from being born and lengthen the travail of its parturition. The sensate world is too far decayed to be aided by their "reforms". In fact, most of their reforms are symptoms and part of the decadence. Such men will multiply the misery of coming generations a hundred fold. The only thing which can now save Western civilization from the permanent annihilation which Spengler foresees for it is a basic change in the tests of value by which men live, is a return to Christian principles in morals, in philosophy, in politics and international relations, in education in government, in society, in home and family, in fact, in every area of human activity and existence. This change is in motion. Nothing will arrest it permanently. The blindness of the materialistic "liberals" before it is impotent to halt the future over long range time. It is sad, indeed, that so many of them willfully close their eyes to it and refuse to see it. For some of them are potentially capable of assuming creative rôles for the future in our return to Christian civilization. This they ought to be doing instead of playing supremely stultifying rôles in their time in trying to prop up sagging sensate values which are honestly past the saving.

Notes to Chapter III

1. This decline is, in fact, paralleled in other fields. A volume now in preparation by the author, *The Reality of Our Decline,* establishes the wide spread progress of the sensate decline in the second half of the nineteenth century..
2. *Cf.* Matthew, XXIII, 13-39.

CHAPTER FOUR

PER ASPERA AD CHRISTUM

Leadership of our New Renaissance

THE NEW RENAISSANCE of the Spirit is already a-borning. It is being led principally by the same countries which led the last Renaissance, by France and Italy. Petrarca and Boccaccio, Giotto and Villon, Marco Polo and Leonardo, Froissart and Marie de France, Abélard, Jean de Meung, Guillaume de Lorris, Michelangelo and Galileo, Rabelais and Columbus, the bankers of Florence and Naples, the sensate troubadours of Provence were the French and Italian leaders of the future hundreds of years ago. They were among the most important establishers of modern tests of value. By their books, their ideas, their art, their songs and poems and lives, they helped spread the modern sensate or pagan tests of value throughout the West. The names of such great Italian and French establishers of the modern world need, of course, to be supplemented by their less numerous contemporaries from so many other lands, from England to Germany and Bohemia, from Chaucer and Wycliffe to Walter von der Vogelweide and Hus. It is doubtful, however, if any group of men did so much to foster the rising values of the senses as did the French troubadours of Provence who spread their pagan ideas over most of Western and Southern Europe. The fact that they have remained usually nameless should not lead us to underestimate their significance: at all times, and especially during transition periods, it is the personalities and influence of men which are most important, not their names.

Today also France and Italy in their literature and thought are often years ahead of any of the other great countries of the West in our New Renaissance of the Spirit just as they were in that of the senses six hundred years ago. Bernadette of Lourdes, Ste. Thérèse of Lisieux, Maritain, Péguy, Bergson, Montalembert, Claudel, Saint-Exupéry, Jammes, Beaudelaire, Rimbaud, Verlaine, Le Cardonnel, Popes Pius XI, Pius XII, Leo XIII are typical examples of French and Italian writers and thinkers who are harbingers of the future. England and Germany are beginning to play also the same rôles they played in the last Renaissance, *i. e.*, they are relatively not holding back the future; they are often beginning to advance it. Germans like Werfel, Borchhardt, Count Bishop von Preysing, Cardinal Faulhaber, Prince Hubertus zu Lowenstein, Pastor Niemöller, and Englishmen and Americo-Englishmen like Newman and Chesterton and Noyes, Belloc and Maynard, T. S. Eliot and Aldous Huxley and Christopher Dawson are traversing the same ground which their French and Italian contemporaries have covered a few years before them.

There is nothing weird or mysterious in the European leadership of our New Renaissance, nor in the fact that it is being frequently led by the Romance nations of the South. The Mediterranean world has been the fountain head and source of all our Renaissances of the past, from that of Greece in the fourth and third centuries B. C.

down through the present one. The Romance and Mediterranean peoples and nations of the South attained great heights in Western civilization fifteen hundred years earlier than even the peoples of Northern Europe. At the same time that the ancestors of the modern inhabitants of England and Scandinavia and Germany and Russia were hide-clad barbarians living in the woods and plain of Northern and Central and Eastern Europe, the ancestors of the modern inhabitants of the Mediterranean world were carving some of the most beautiful sculpture, building some of the most sublime architecture, writing some of the finest poetry and drama, pondering some of the most profound ideas which Western man has ever produced. This fifteen hundred years' start which the Mediterranean peoples have over those of the North of Europe is hard to overcome. It has, in fact, never yet been completely overcome in many areas. The externals of civilization in food and dress, in bearing and demeanor, that intangible *savoir vivre*, the deep knowledge of what life is and how to live it, are still often better upheld by the Mediterranean peoples than by their Germanic and Slavonic neighbors. Then, too, the Roman Empire did much to establish and define the limits of what belongs preëminently to the leadership of Western civilization. It left a permanent impress upon the lands which belonged most intimately to its world. To them it gave not only its language but also its disciplines, its laws, its standards and habits of thought; even in its hour of decay it passed on to the future the church of Christendom; Rome, the eternal, even when it lost the sensate leadership of the West, was its spiritual head. Predominantly sensate Rome was deeply rooted enough in Western civilization, in fact, sufficiently *identical* with it, to pass on even to a spiritual future the organization of the universal church, its language, and frequently its leadership.

Among the great creative nations of modern history, France and Italy most convincingly bear the standards of Western civilization because they most thorougly among the modern nations belonged to the great Roman Empire. They most thoroughly know what Western civilization is and means, represent it most adequately. Also belonging to the Roman Empire, and, therefore, to Western civilization were England and Spain and Germany. England and Spain and even more so Germany, however, were the fringes of the Roman Empire in comparison with France and Italy; the effects of their not always belonging so intimately to Western civilization are still traceable today. There are still occasional twists and quirks in Spanish and English and German character which are not completely in harmony with the traditions of the West.

Among these are the mercantile aggressiveness of the English and the Germans, their limitless eagerness to acquire, their warlike tenacity, their unyielding stubbornness, their awkward reserve or social self-consciousness, and, most decisive of all, their cloudy romantic mysticism compounded of the undispelled fogs of the North and the lingering remnants of Nordic and druidic paganism. The Germans and English have an adolescent thirst and yearning like school children to "stand first" in the world which the wiser maturity of the Romance peoples has long since abandoned as being unworthy of deeply civilized men. Besides, Christianity, the most important element of Western civilization, came to England and Germany hundreds of years later than it did to the Romance South and has not yet had time to root itself so deeply as it has in Italy or France. In fact, the Christianity of the

North, weakened and distorted by the Protestant Revolt, has quite other roots and has put forth quite different branches from the older Catholicity of the South. In the North it became more secularized and split up into rival impotent groups which fell under the power of the state or subjected themselves to the state, with even a totalitarian tendency to become tools of the state and of the social and economic platitudes of the state. In other aspects it became a state religion as Anglicanism in England, Lutheranism in Scandinavia and Imperial Germany, the Reformed Church in the Netherlands, much as Orthodox Christianity did among the Slavonic peoples. Or worse yet, the secularization went so far in the Protestant New World as to separate entirely church and state and not give even lip service to the idea that the affairs of government and the social order might have some connection with the affairs of God. In contrast, the Christianity of the Romance South insisted, at least, theoretically, on the primacy of first things. Even if not always able to effect a proper earthly order it at least emphasized an ideal separation of church and state in the affairs which could be clearly delineated as purely spiritual and purely secular but in those which might be mixed proposed that the government of God should take precedence over that of man, that the higher order should prevail over the lower, that the yardstick of eternity measure over that of temporality.

As for the Spaniard, his intermingling for centuries with the Saracens is the principal source of his lack of complete Westernization in comparison with that of the Frenchman or Italian. For seven hundred years Spain almost unaided absorbed the blows of the Moors against Western civilization. Spain saved the West for seven centuries. The debt of the West to Spain is gigantic. But in her absorptive martyrdom for the West she ceased in part to belong to it; for this mighty sacrifice, mightier than that of any other modern nation, not even excepting Ireland or Poland, she has had somewhat weakened the other rôles she has played in Western civilization. Had it not been for her seven centuries of intimate contact with the Moor, Spain would probably belong as completely to the West as Italy or France, for she belonged quite integrally to the Roman Empire and shares with them the languge and tradition and Christian truth of Rome.

Only a mad-man, or a hopeless Romano-phile, would deny that Germany and England and Spain belong to the leadership of the West. No one can seriously question the fact that frequently their contributions to the West are as great as those of Italy or France. But they are not as sustained. They do not have the unbroken creative loyalty to the leadership in Western tradition which Italy and France possess. They were the fringe countries of the Roman Empire; to a certain extent they remain the fringe countries in the leadership of Western civilization in our Renaissance today as they did in the Renaissance of six hundred years ago. They belong, and belong nobly, to Western civilization; but it cannot be convincingly maintained that England and Germany and Spain belong as intensely and as creatively to the West as do France and Italy. It is even possible that the most creative rôles of Western civilization belong *permanently* to Italy and to France, to the Greco-Romano-Mediterranean world. France and Italy are in a literal sense the only classical nations in the West to survive into modern times. It is the classical spirit and tradition in literature and art, in thought and architecture, which express most admirably what is often called the aesthetic best in Western culture. Moreover, it is France and Italy alone of the major modern nations of the West which adhere to the most sacred principle of Western civilization, its holy, universal church. Secularism and paganism in these lands as everywhere in the West have made terrible inroads. But of them alone among modern major nations it is still barely possible to say "Catholic France, Catholic Italy."

What of the West lay beyond the borders of the Roman Empire—the outer Germans, the Slavs, and the New World—belongs to the creative leadership of the West even less than England, Germany, or Spain. Such lands will have to go through hundreds, and perhaps thousands of years of loyalty to the West to which they are as yet only beginning to belong before they possess the intensity of Westernization which marks France and Italy. The most effective way in which such areas, be they Slavonic or New Worldish or Asiatic, can really develop an eminently Western spirit is by the utmost loyalty to the spirit and principles of Christianity, the noblest, purest element in Western tradition. To that degree any area is Christian, to that it may be spoken of as belonging most nobly to the West. To that degree to which it is not Christian it plays a backward rôle in our New Renaissance. To that degree to which it is materialistic, pagan, mechanistic, to that degree it is backward in our time. Romance, Catholic France and Italy, often purged of materialism and mechanism beyond the Slav and Germanic world, trusting not to the sword and the might of armies, and rarely as greedy and bellicose world-acquirers as their Germanic English and German neighbors, in men like Péguy and Claudel and Bergson and Maritain and Pius XII lead the Renaissance of today as they did that of many hundred years ago through Petrarca and Boccaccio and Villon and Rabelais.

Russia too is seemingly playing in our New Renaissance the same old rôle as always, that of being five hundred years behind the times. Now that the sensate world has begun to decay, Russia has joined the sensate world as a convinced epigone half a millennium late. It is questionable to what degree Russia really belongs to Western civilization or is capable of playing any rôle of leadership in it. There are, and always have been in recent centuries, two currents of thought in Russia itself with regard to this question. Great Russian historians such as Karisheff, Klyuchevski, Kareyeff, Vernadski consider these two opposite currents of thought and feeling as determinative in Russian history.

One group of Russians, typified by Peter the Great and Lenin (and after Peter frequently called the Petroffs), have wanted to belong to the West and have conscientiously bent their efforts to force Russia into patterns which they at least sincerely thought were Western. They have always been a small minority among influential Russians with the result that their influence has in the main been superficial and transitory. Most of the Russian intellectuals for the past three centuries have belonged to the other camp, that of the Slavonophiles. The Slavonophiles hate Europe and the West, turn their face eastward to Asia, insist that Russia is and should be an Asiatic country, that her contacts with the West should be minimal. Dostoievski, who is without doubt Russia's greatest literary genius, although probably, because of his occasional tendencies toward Slavonophilism, not as well known in the West as his much inferior contemporary Tolstoi,

158

expresses very concisely the Slavonophile gospel with both its contempt and hatred of the West as well as its worship for Russia and Asia:

"Europe, what is it? A graveyard, filled, maybe, with expensive tombstones, but filled likewise with the stench of corruption, its contents not even fit to serve as dung for the new seed! This new seed can blossom only on Russian soil. What are the French? Vain fops! And the Germans? A base nation of sausage makers. The English? Hawkers of a crude rationalism. The Jews? They stink of pride. Catholicism? The doctrine of the devil and an insult to Christ. Protestantism? The mockery of the one true faith, a rationalistic state religion, crusher of freedom and men's souls, leading to a tyrant state domineering over its subjects. . . . . [Western] cities are Babylon, the great whore of the Apocalypse. . . . All the ideas Europe has given birth to are no more than a bunch of faded flowers fit only for the dust bin. Science is a vain delusion. Democracy is the skilly of persons suffering from softening of the brain. Revolution is a puppet show of fools born or fools made. Pacifism is an old wives' tale. The Russian idea is alone great and true and right. . . . We Russians are omnicomprehending. You [Westerners] are narrow minded and limited. Russia alone, with all that is in her, is good and right; tsar and knout, orthodox priest and peasant, troika and ikon; and these things acquire additional rightness the more they are anti-European, the more they are Asiatic, Mongolian, Tartar, the more they are conservative, retrogressive, unprogressive, unintellectual, Byzantine. . . . Let us be Asiatics. . . . Away from Petersburg, the European city; back to Moscow and Siberia! . . . . Russia is the dogma which must be accepted without questioning. Russia cannot be understood by means of the rational faculties; it can be understood only through faith. He who refuses to bend the knee to this new dogma is a foe, is anti-Christ. A crusade must be preached against the enemies of mankind. Austria must be trampled under foot; the crescent must be torn from St. Sophia's in Constantinople. Germany must be humbled and England vanquished. . . . The whole world must come under Russia's hegemony that the kingdom of God may be established."

It is interesting to note that three out of the four European "enemies of mankind" whom Dostoievski flayed have already received the scourging he prophesied for them only three quarters of a century ago. Dostoievski is not a particularly violent Slavonophile. In fact, he is a relatively mild one and in many important respects scarcely a Slavonophile at all. Yet, the anti-European note of his gospel sounds extremely violent to Western ears. The innocents in the Western world, particularly numerous in England and America, who think it is going to be so easy to absorb Russia into a common brotherhood of the West, simply are blindly ignorant of the fact that the Slavonophile mind is the normal one in Russia, that the *zapadnyiki,* those who wish Russia to belong to the West, and not to Asia and the East, are the exception, not the rule.

The Slavonophiles are intensely national, are thoroughly devoted to "mother Russia", and contend that Russia invariably suffers from her contacts with the West, that she should guard against them, should be eternally suspicious of the West, should divest herself of every trace of Westernization. The first important division between Lenin and Trotsky on the one hand and Stalin on the other had its roots in the *zapadnyiki*-Slavonophile conflict. Lenin and Trotsky, leaning to the West, held that Communism had come from the West and should be returned to the West as soon as possible by internal revolutions even at the peril and sacrifice of Russia if need be. They held that Communism was greater than Russia, that Russia should strain herself to the utmost for the world cause. Stalin, the Slavonophile, held that the first duty of Communist Russia was to make herself strong so that no one might assault her victoriously, that the first duty of Russia was to Russia, not to Communism. As has been regular in Russian history, the

Slavonophiles won out over the Leninites and Trotsky·ites, the *zapadnyiki*, even in Communism; and even more determinedly than the tsars, the Stalinites turned their faces toward Asia and built up within a generation in Asia the mighty industrial and agricultural machine which enabled them in our day to lose the most significant parts of European Russia and still absorb the worst blows of the German invader and eventually to hurl him back into the "evil West" from which he came.

In spite of superficial appearances to the contrary, and the very loose thinking which these have engendered, Russia in World War II has moved further than ever into Asia. In the twentieth century she will as usual probably play a very minor rôle in terms of creative leadership of Western culture, a much smaller rôle, in fact, than she did in the last half of the nineteenth century. By her military might alone she will cut a figure in the West in our time, and in that sense probably only a negative rôle. For military might does not give creative leadership to any Renaissance and is particularly inappropriate in a spiritual one. Invaded, divided, struggling, bickering, weak chaotic Italy and France gave the leadership to the West six hundred years ago in the last Renaissance. How similar, even almost identical, is the military and political rôle they play in the present one! Not by legions alone does one control or even influence the world. The warning of Christ, the leader and establisher of the last Renaissance of the spirit, might well be heeded by the shepherds of nations today who think that in military power and wealth and prestige and police force lie the keys to the future: to Peter, who had cut off the ear of the servant of the high priest, came His rebuking reminder: "Put back thy sword; for all those who take the sword shall perish by the sword."

Because the Russians have come in latest to the industrialization and mechanization of our declining sensate culture, in fact, have joined it only at a time when it has lost its creativity and is already degenerate, not having had a chance to know sensatism at its best, they will cling to it longest and in its worst form. Russia will do the most of any of the great nations of the West, or near-West, to halt and delay the future. The Russians in spite of what they think is their fine modernity and progressivism, or, perhaps, *because* of it, will be playing the ordinary backward rôle which Russia has always played in the West to which she only most superficially belongs. What creative rôles Russia has to offer in our New Renaissance of the Spirit will be through the influence of individual Russian writers and thinkers rather than the rôle of a nation as a whole. Through these she certainly has a part to offer and is indeed offering it. Beyond these she will offer little but "liberal" and sensate reaction. Her recent national program of atheism, her present one of anti-Catholicity, completely unfit her from any national creative rôle in a New Renaissance of the Spirit and if persisted in rob her of whatever minor chance she might have had to participate actively in it.

There are, however, at least three individual modern Russian figures who have played what will prove to be among the most significant rôles of any men of the nineteenth and twentieth centuries in creating and interpreting the New World of the Spirit. These men are Dostoievski, Berdyaev, and Sorokin. Berdyaev and Sorokin are exiles from Russia and are, perhaps, helped by their very contrast with their nation and their absence from it. Although Russian, they represent almost nothing of the contemporary forces which mislead Russia. Berdyaev will rank as one of the greatest spiritual philosophers of the twentieth century. Sorokin more clearly than any other man, not excepting even Spengler, has understood our time as an age of convulsion and transition from one set of values to another, has done more than any writer to date to state the issues and the solutions of our age. Dostoievski is the first writer of world importance to belong as a transition figure to the new civilization of the spirit. A full generation before Péguy and Bernadette of Lourdes or Newman, Dostoievski had broken with the sensate past and was speaking of and creating the new world of the Spirit.

Since he was the first important harbinger of the new world, Dostoievski did not understand too clearly what he represented. He was frequently a confusing and a confused figure. Much of his break with the sensate past was an indirect result of his tendency to Slavonophilism. He hated Europe and what Europe represented and understood bitterly the inadequacy and hypocrisy of his time, comprehended the inadequacy and shallowness and failure of a world based in the senses and materialism and secularism. A man of intense honesty, hostile to inadequacy, he was angered at what he saw around him much as Christ was; and he lashed out savagely against it as had Christ when He drove the materialists out of the temple with His stinging whip. Dostoievski belongs clearly to the future by his comprehension of the failure of science to solve any of the moral, intellectual, or physical problems of the world and the spiritual and physical bankruptcy to which it would bring the world; in his insight into the failure and bankruptcy of rationalism, relativism, liberalism, and secularism; in his comprehension of the mass tyranny to which these forces would lead; in his understanding of the inadequacy of a world based in the poor, obfuscated senses of humanity; in his comprehension of the imminence of a spiritual renaissance; and, above all, in his knowledge that the answers to all the problems of the world can be found in Christ and Christ alone. He came almost three quarters of a century before Spengler and Sorokin. Unlike them, however, he had little understanding of the sweep of things and the rôles of nations in the New Renaissance of the Spirit. He was so rooted in Russia that his tendency toward Slavonophilism clouded his vision, most lamentably of all toward the true nature of Western culture and its best expression in Western Catholic Christendom. In spite of these inadequacies Dostoievski is one of the supremely great moderns, as much a pioneer of his time as was in his day St. Stephan, the first martyr of Christianity, or Giotto or Petrarch or Boccaccio, those moulders of modernity, were in their fourteenth century. He, Berdyaev, and Sorokin are Russia's greatest contributions to the future in individual rôles. They are among the very greatest men of their time.

The United States and, in fact, the whole group of nations of the Western hemisphere are, like Russia, playing no very significant creative rôle in the New Renaissance of the Spirit. They are sometimes playing even a very backward one. The New World had no possible rôle to play in the last Renaissance. It was not even yet discovered, had not yet begun to belong to the West. At the present time the most significant rôle America seems to be playing is through her very existence. She does more by being than by doing. She is a symbol for all who suffer that there is a place on earth where, even if many things are far from ideal, at least some of the extremes of cruelty of man to man are fortunately absent. In the minds of the oppressed and suffering everywhere America has for centuries stood as a symbol of escape. She gave hope by which men have held on to life, have been saved from the slough of despair. Even if she had not produced one of the world's great literatures, if her art and music and culture did not measure up to European levels, America for centuries has offered an asylum for the aching bodies and tortured hearts of those who fled from some of the more extreme sensate inadequacies or cruelties of the old world. America has in this sense a mighty place in the leadership of the West in terms of hope. One of the things which the West needs very much is obviously hope. America can give this and give it richly. Yet, there is even a highly inadequate note in the hope America offers. Unfortunately for a New Renaissance of the Spirit her hope has been largely a hope in sensate values, of values resting in the primacy of life, hope for higher standards of living, hope for greater material blessings, hope for greater freedom of activity within the areas of sensate existence which sensate men have held important. In the hope that America has been holding out to the world there has always been too little realization of the profundity of truth which lay in Christ's statement. "My kingdom is not of this world". America's kingdom has been uniquely in this world. Its existence has been predominantly sensate, barring the people of genuinely spiritual religious conviction who came to the New World. Even those who superficially seem to have come to America principally for religious reasons were when viewed dispassionately often more deeply spurred on by materialistic reasons than by spiritual ones. It is not without a certain inner logic inherent in our existence from earliest Puritanical days that Anglo-

Saxon America has become one of the most intensely materialistic areas that have ever existed in the world. Puritanism was essentially no more a religious movement than it was a political and economic one; and the Puritans came to the New World seeking religious elbow room perhaps even less eagerly than an opportunity for economic development. The Puritan soul was *a priori* always anti-Christian enough to see its most harmonious development in that way of life where it could make the most money. Anglo-Saxon America, with so much of its temperament and so many of its attitudes and standards set by the Puritans, never had a Christian chance. Religion and money making, the insistence of God's Kingdom being very definitely and profitably rooted in this world, were so inextricably woven together that it is not without profound inner reason that Anglo-Saxon America has never known too clearly what genuine Christianity is. Nor is it strange that, with materialism so inextricably intertwined with its religious roots, America can usually find money-making more profitable and interesting than religion. The Anglo-Saxon American at his best can unfortunately often be summed up in the supposed words of a Bostonian philosopher: "When I can do a good action and at the same time make money, I feel that all my powers are moving in harmonious concentration." The sensate overtone has been more dominant in Anglo-Saxon America than it has in the French and Portuguese and Spanish areas to the north and south of the Anglo-Saxon culture pocket. Its almost exclusively sensate existence, the fact that it has known no other historical period than a sensate one, singularly unfits America for a place of great leadership in a Renaissance of the Spirit.

Yet, because Anglo-Saxon Americans have had so

much, they are often big hearted, generous beyond all peoples. Who, even in the Christian Middle Ages, ever gave away so much unselfishly as do Americans, and little, plain everyday Americans even more than our leaders and big wealthy Americans? For the latter are so often motivated by that most un-Christian of all gospels—"enlightened self-interest". The plain Anglo-Saxon American, because he has had so much, will give and give unselfishly when appeal is made to him. America, plain, everyday America, has often fed and clothed those who yesterday were almost unknown to her, heathen, Christian, demi-Christian, and former foe alike. America has given away more than some nations have ever had—and given it almost with no thought of return, save the satisfaction of helping those who were in need. We in America often lack a pettiness of spirit that others so intensely possess. We will haggle less over a million than others would over a penny.

Perhaps, the most significant rôle America is playing in the present Renaissance is to give at various times in the twentieth century a place of temporary exile and physical sustenance to some of the great expatriates of our time like Maritain or Sorokin or Werfel, and in less terrible periods feed them and their brother millions in their homelands. What America is doing for them is very helpful and will be gratefully remembered. It is sometimes hard in the terrible chaos and convulsion of transition to keep alive the spark of life in the leaders of a movement. America in our time has helped greatly in making this possible both by asylum on its own soil and its charities and sacrifices abroad. This is, perhaps, not an entirely essential rôle. The future will not die regardless of what happens physically to some of its leaders. Dostoievski would say that it is only out of suffering that the new life can be born.

But, in another sense, what is done for our fellow men, even for the least of them, is done for Christ. America, thus, often works for Christ even when she is not entirely clear for Whom she is working. It is another example of the leavening effect of the Christian gospel. A little bit of leaven, in this case that of charity for our fellow man, is potentially capable of making us one of the most creative spreaders of the Christian gospel. We partake in a movement of whose end goal we have almost no inkling. We throw material bread upon the waters and it will return to us some day in the form of spiritual sponge cake. We build the world of the spirit participatingly and creatively and sometimes we see in our action no more than a caring for the physical bodies of men. God is really at work in those who do even a little for Him. In His own good time He will help us of Anglo-Saxon America into a greater wisdom than seemed possible for us rooted, as so much of our nation is, in the confused murk of Puritanism.

Hopeful in this direction also is the admirable growth in numbers and influence of Catholics in America, who in their homeland can be among the most creative forces in enabling America to participate in the leadership of a New Renaissance of the Spirit. If Puritanism with its confused and muddled philosophy has deprived America in the past of Christian and intellectual leadership in the world, it can be hoped for the not too distant future that American Catholic intellectuals, rooted in the clear thinking of Aristotle and Aquinas and following the admirable rational spirit of Christianity, will take their place among the most formative influences of their time in leading the entire Western world toward God.

Beyond this present provision for the physical sustenance of some of the most creative men of our time, the Werfels, Sorokins, Maritains, Koestlers, and beyond the hope that Catholicity gives America for growing leadership, our nation is seemingly at the moment offering little to the leadership of the future, in one sense scarcely even as much as Russia. For those writers who belong in whole or in part to the New Renaissance whom America might claim as her very own, men like T. S. Eliot or Hutchins or Santayana or Babbitt, seem to prefer to ally themselves with the movement in England or Italy or France or Germany. It is always a sad spectacle to see a number of a nation's creative writers sink their roots abroad or even in some instances go to live abroad and adopt foreign citizenship. It is doubly tragic when they do this as voluntary expatriates driven by no terrible upheaval or threat of death. It is understandable that trite reiterators of the commonplace like Whitman or Steinbeck or Sandburg or Hemingway or R. B. Perry or Whitehead or Dewey should feel at home in America. But it puts us back generations when Eliot or Santayana or Babbitt depart physically or spiritually from us.

America, like Russia, belongs preëminently to the inadequate sensate world of the past. Like Russia she has faith in machines and dams, in power, in industry, in armies and sea-fleets and air-fleets, in international police forces and restraints and financial agreements, in science and materialism and mechanism and "modernism" and secularism when the creative forces of the world are sick unto death of machines and dams and power and industry and armies. From a number of important approaches, however, it is doubtful if America is quite as backward in the Renaissance of the Spirit as Russia. Although not a Christian country even in nominal church membership, with fifty-two per cent of its population not even giving lip service adherence to any religious group, in spite of its blatant secularism and paganism, America, at least as yet, has not entered upon any government controlled and sponsored anti-God program as has Russia in recent years. Secondly, the common language and literature and tradition we share with England will help to drag us along toward the Renaissance of the Spirit whether we want it or not. Lastly, the whole New World belongs to Western civilization more closely than Russia. We have never had to fend entirely for ourselves. We have always drunk rather deeply of the inspiration of Western civilization from England or Spain or France or Germany or Portugal. We have never been isolated from Western culture to the same degree to which Russia frequently is. The mother countries of England and Spain and France and Portugal gave the New World their languages, their literatures, their culture, part of their very being. Independence from the mother countries has fortunately always been partly an illusion. In the twentieth century our country has dutifully and obediently returned to the common-fold of the British Commonwealth as if it had never left it. This association with England in her language and culture and tradition will probably save the United States from playing the most reactionary rôle for the future of any of the great nations of the West. A similar situation holds in varying degree for the Latin nations of the New World in their closeness to their Romance mothers.

Nor do Asia and Africa as continents have probably any major creative rôles for the immediate future except to that degree to which their inclusion in the world of

France and England or their Christian roots may bring them in touch with the persons and the spirit of the Renaissance. The coming world of the spirit will be a Christian civilization. To the degree to which an area is Christian it will have a major rôle to play in the dawning Renaissance of our time. If Asia and Africa should become more Christian than the West, the West will have passed on to them the most important element in Western civilization and they will become its leaders. Western civilization is not principally a matter of color or of geography; in fact, it is not these at all; but rather it is a matter of ideas. The most important idea of the West is Christianity. But for the immediate Renaissance geography is still important, for Asia and Africa are not yet Christian to any considerable degree. The Renaissance of our time will arise in the West, its leadership will remain there for foreseeable time. It may bring greater benefits to non-Western areas than did the last three Renaissances. In the first place, the evangelization of the East and of Africa may very possibly proceed at a rate hitherto unparalleled. The sensate world with its scientific marvels of radio and airplane and fast-moving ships provides the media by which the gospel of Christ can be quickly and efficiently brought to the whole world if only such media can be controlled by proper values. The radio, the airplane, the swift ships are morally indifferent in themselves. They are forces for good *or* evil, depending entirely on the will and the intentions of those who use them. They are equally capable of sowing hate and destruction and war and misery or the gospel of Christ. Enough of modern facility in communications may survive the convulsions of the next generations so that the Asiatic and African, areas formerly severed both in body and spirit from the

West by vast geographical expanse will be closely joined with the West. Only time will tell whether the severity of the transition will eradicate the results of applied science and technology or not. It is certain that the results of applied science and technology must soon cease to become ends in themselves. They must equally cease to serve decadent sensate ends. They must be harmonized and fused with the arising values of the spirit and made to serve principally spiritual ends if they are to live through the period of transition. If modern communications survive in whole or in part, our new Western Renaissance will potentially affect the non-Western areas more strikingly than before, and knit them with the West as one unit under God. In the second place, the new Renaissance may affect non-Western areas more strongly than previous renaissances, for Asia in particular may be more susceptible to influence from a Western spiritual world than it ever could be to the clangor and expediency and mechanism and superficial agitation of a Western sensate world. What Asia has been unwilling to accept from a mechanized West, which it has in part despised, in part pitied, and in part envied, it might very readily accept from a respritualized West. It was precisely because the West was poor in the spirit in which Asia has often been rich that the West has been a relative failure in Asia in spite of modern communications.

Yet, the African and Asiatic areas will not play an independent or major creative part in the New Renaissance. They are too old, too rigid, too used up, in addition to belonging too little to Christianity. They are not independent enough of the powerful nations of the West, nor will they so become. These areas can change their masters, drive one out, as for example the British from

India or the French from Syria or the Dutch from Indo-
nesia. This they can and probably will do. But if they do,
they will succumb to another master, for example, Russia.
This is, in fact, the probable trend of the future. Russia
will be drawn more and more into Asia, will belong progressively less to the West, and with Asia will do little
to advance the New Renaissance. Nor will the areas of
Asia and Africa in foreseeable time produce a really independent existence of their own. Even the form of their
present sullen rebelliousness, togther with its aims, is a reflection of the present sensate decadence of the West, is
imported from Western Europe and Washington and Moscow. These areas constitute in the main objects and war
resources for the decadent Western powers; their countries
are battlefields for the battles of the exploding Western
powers and the New World. What importance they may
achieve for the moment in this direction, great as it may
be, is transitory. Far from being leaders of the New
Renaissance these areas will probably remain reactionary
and decadent longer than any of the nations of the West,
not even excepting Russia. Russia and, to a certain extent,
America, will probably transmit to Asia the decadent
sensate phase of mechanism and technology after these as
ends in themselves have become only a memory in Europe.
Then Asia will be deep in the decadence of a sensate
world centuries after Europe will have swung into its
spiritual future.

More important still, Western civilization by its resiliency differs in its fundamental nature from the civilizations of the East. When Western civilization becomes
decadent and non-creative in one form, it changes to a
quite opposite form. Its resiliency, one of its most remark-

able qualities, is the outward expression of the rise and fall of the sensate and spiritual forms. Western civilization did not die twenty-five hundred years ago in the spiritual decline of Old Greece; it did not die with the passing of sensate Rome; nor with the passing of the Middle Ages; nor will it die with the passing of modern times. In its times of decadence it changes its tests of value and acquires new and vigorous life. It is tough and resilient. But when an Eastern civilization decays, it remains frozen for millennia in its decadence. It lacks the forces of self-renewal and self-perpetuation which Western civilization so resiliently possesses. Such petrifacts as Egypt, India, China may continue to exist as they are for hundreds of thousands of years, dead bodies, non-creative, amorphous, dispirited masses of men, scrap material from a once great history. The century old "Fellaheen" nations of India and China in their static, frozen civilization form a striking contrast to the Antaean-like ability of the Western Mediterranean world to renew itself. For three thousand years the Mediterranean world has been the cradle for the creative tests of value of the West. Renaissance after Renaissance it has inspired new strength and vigor into Western civilization. No matter how decadent one type of world might become in the West, a new type of world sprang into being. Asia and Africa occasionally contributed personages like Augustine or Paul who became leaders in the various renaissances of the West. They did not give the soil of fruition. Final creativity was not theirs. It is not otherwise now. The new Renaissance of the Spirit is a western movement. Its leadership is principally in the hands of the leaders of the last Renaissance, France and Italy, and less so, England and Germany. It is not to be found principally elsewhere.

Comprehension of our age by Spengler

Because our is a time of Renaissance, of a complete shift of values, of a clean sweep away from the past into the future, the fundamental nature of our age needs to be stressed again and again. The men of our time like those of any Renaissance are like children in school: they need constant repetition of what is being taught and they need teachers who will pour all that they can into their work to help their pupils understand. The men of our time need to be told and retold what is the nature of the epoch in which they live, and they need to be told by as many people as possible. For each who comprehends something of his time can comprehend it only in part. The finite vision of any single man is too limited to catch all the vastness of the volcanic upheavals which are refashioning the world. We can see only darkly as through a glass what coming generations will see face to face. The author is quite aware, therefore, that in many respects there is no new point of view in this book. What it says has been hinted at and partly covered by Sorokin and Spengler and to a lesser extent by Ortega y Gasset, Hayek, Claudel, Toynbee, Dostoievski, and Péguy. Yet, the author makes no apology for repeating what has been said before. He may not say it as well as many others. But inevitably he will bring into greater relief and clarity areas which have hitherto been in relative shadow. The interpretation of this book is new. Its emphasis is different from that of its predecessors. It is hoped so also will be its effect. The writer in the same breath admits his indebtedness to the thinkers who have so clearly understood their time as well as claims his independence from them.

Oswald Spengler, unlike most of the small fry thinkers

of our time, has reached great heights by making the
necessary severance from the liberalistic, materialistic outlook which has been the curse of Western civilization
through its great writers since the French Revolution and
in lesser degree since the Protestant Revolt and the Renaissance itself. In doing so Spengler has understood the
seriousness of the crisis of our time as well as any man
of his age excepting perhaps Sorokin. He has fallen, however, into the unfortunate pessimism which has blurred the
vision and marred the thinking of other great German
philosophers since Schopenhauer and he has come to
understand only one phase of our time, the incontrovertible festering of decay in contemporary Western civilization. He has likened Western civilization itself to a biological organism and has attributed to it a birth, an
infancy, an adolescence, a maturity, and a senectitude into
which it is now well advanced, and a not too distant death.
He would wrongly have us believe that civilization be-
haves like any animal organism; once born it will die, be
remembered a while, and then forgotten. Spengler in his
boundless pessimism sends us permanently and irrevocably
into destruction. He bears incontrovertible witness to our
decline and like a laboratory observer he interests himself in our convulsions dispassionately and concludes that
we shall soon descend into the nether world of annihilation, either never to rise again or at so late a date as to
have lost the continuity of Western history.

Through his German pessimism Spengler falls into
four errors. First, he is wrong in equating Western civilization to a biological organism. Secondly, in denying free
will he denies our freedom of action and makes us hopeless puppets of our time. Thirdly, he is at fault in underestimating our resiliency, even the toughness of our civil-

ization. Lastly, he is so intent on observing the increasing twilight of our declining world of things that he fails utterly to see the real, creative trend of the future, the dawn of values of the spirit. Like Schopenhauer and Nietzsche he has caught half the world and missed the other and certainly more important half—the Renaissance of Christianity, of religion perhaps of every sort, of the eternal, of the supernatural, the triumph of spirit, of soul, of God.

His effect has been, in part, bad. He has fathered a spirit of hopelessness, of pessimism, of inertia. Had he been fired with the vision of a medieval churchman, he might well have been the Thomas Aquinas of his age. As it is, he will be doubtless remembered and honored for centuries. His essential greatness, however, has been marred by his dismal pessimism. Spengler has a studied dispassionateness, even aloofness from his time characteristic of romantic German pessimists. He sees Western civilization plunging into what seems to him permanent ruin. He observes, surveys, and placidly consigns us to destruction. He betrays in no way that he *belongs* to Western civilization, that it is *his* world too which is exploding. Like a Martian come to observe our chaos, he stands aloof, and with the indifference of the Teutonic gods to their fate, he dispassionately and stoically condemns us to perish hopelessly, helplessly. He has pagan Stoic grandeur, Teutonic, silent, dutiful devotion to the "inevitable", what one might call *pflichtvolle Verschwiegenheit*. He is the unyielding, unhumble, arrogant pagan.

Our time—and the future—none the less owes him one mighty debt on the score of having brought to its attention the seriousness of the impending crisis. While the blindling liberals, the evolutionists, the pseudo-scientists, the economists, the politicians and political experts, the leaders of nations, of industry, of the arts, of science, and of literature were generally misled by the errors of the eighteenth and nineteenth centuries, by Rousseauism, by Darwinism, secularism, by exaggerated and ill-conceived concepts of progress and evolution, and were preaching the dawn of everything good and marvellous was just around the corner, when, in reality, we were plunging into the greatest wars, revolutions, human miseries of all time, Spengler understood the disintegration of the West, and raised his voice to tell the truth as he clearly but inadequately perceived it. Few men even today realize the greatness and the truth of Spengler. He is of the future because he saw and heralded the impotence, the decay, even the foulness of our time. His pessimism, his lack of faith were his stumbling blocks. Civilization is not, as he believes, comparable to a biological organism. It need not, and does not, subject itself to solely biological laws. He neglected Godhead. He overloked free will. Nor is Western civilization so easily led to the slaughter block as Spengler believed. It is of an unbelievable resiliency because of the innate creativeness and resourcefulness of Western man. He creates a new world when the old one proves inadequate. He does not meekly fold his hands and perish with it. Yet, in spite of his obvious deficiencies Spengler dwarfs most of his contemporaries. He comes close to having the real sweep of things. How much closer is his work to truth than were the sayings and writings of those who considered themselves and were considered as the philosophic and literary sources of truth just before the first World War when Spengler was writing his *Untergang des Abendlandes!* How much closer was he to truth than were Dewey and Whitehead, Perry and Russell,

Wells and Tolstoi, Zola and Sumner and Lester Ward. If we subtract the certain monstrous errors which arise from his pessimism and lack of faith, even the slightest amount of quotation from him gives insight into his vision:

"Let it be realized then . . . that the nineteenth and twentieth centuries hitherto looked upon us as the highest point of an ascending straight line of world history, are in reality a stage of life which may be observed in every culture that has ripened to the limit; . . . that inasmuch as our time represents a transitional phase which occurs with certainty under particular conditions. . . . the future of Europe is not a limitless tending upwards and onwards for all time towards our present ideals, but a single phenomenon of history strictly limited and defined as to form and duration, which covers a few centuries, and, can be viewed, and, in essentials calculated, from available precedents. . . . Up to now everyone has been at liberty to hope what he pleased about the future. Where there are no facts, sentiment rules. But henceforward it will be everyone's business to inform himself of what can happen and of what, therefore, with the unalterable necessity of destiny and irrespective of personal ideals, hopes, or desires, will happen. When we use the risky word 'freedom', we shall mean freedom to do not this or that as we may want, but freedom to do the necessary or nothing. . . To birth belongs death, to youth age, to life generally its form and alloted span. . . . This may be deplorable and may well be deplored in pessimist philosophy and poetry, but it is not in our power to make it otherwise. . . . We have to reckon with the hard, cold facts of a late life to which the parallel is to be found . . . in Caesar's Rome. . . . Of great painting and great music there can no longer be for Western people any question. Their architectural possibilities have been exhausted these hundred years". (Introduction to *Decline of the West,* pp. 38-40)

"Consider the decline of art and failing authority of science; the grave problems arising out of the victory of the large cities over the country, such as childlessness and land depopulation; the place in society of a fluctuating fourth estate; the crisis in materialism, in Socialism, parliamentary government; the position of the individual *vis a vis* the state; the problem of private property and the pendant [*sic?*] of marriage." (*Ibid.,* p. 48)

"Only *extensive* possibilities are left for the West. In this phenomenal form our destiny is now irrevocably set. And thus I see in Cecil Rhodes the first man of a new age. . . . His phrase, 'expansion is everything', is the Napoleonic reassertion of the indwelling tendency of *every* civilization which has ripened. It is not a matter of choice, it is not the conscious will of individuals, or even that of whole classes or peoples that decides. The expansive tendency is a doom, something daemonic and immense, which grips, forces into its service, and finally destroys the decadent mankind of our megalopolitan type of civilization willy-nilly, aware or unaware. Hard as the half-developed Socialism of today is fighting against expansion, one day it will become arch-expansionist with all the vehemence of destiny. . . . All this, broad and imposing, is the prelude of a future which is still in store for us and with which the history of mankind will be definitely *closed*. He who does not understand that this outlook is obligatory and insusceptible of modification, that our choice between willing this and willing nothing at all, has no alternative; we either cling to this destiny or despair of the future and life itself. . . . He who is obsessed with the idealism of a provincial and would pursue the ways of life of past ages must forego all desire to comprehend history, to live through history, or to make history." (*Ibid.*, 45-48)

"I offer no wish-picture of the future . . . but a clear picture of the facts as they are and will be. I see further than others. I see not only great possibilities but also great dangers, their origin and perhaps the way to avoid them; and if no one else has the courage to see and to tell what he sees, I mean to do so. . . . That which must happen will happen. A decisive series of events has been set in train. Nothing that has once become a fact can be withdrawn. We are thereafter obliged to walk in the particular direction whether we will or not. It would be short-sighted and cowardly to say no. What the individual will not do, that history will do with him." (*Hour of Decision*, Introduction, XIV)

"We live in momentous times. The stupendous dynamism of the historical epoch that has now dawned makes it the grandest . . . in all world history, greater and by far more terrible than the ages of Caesar and Napoleon. Yet, how blind are the human beings over whom this mighty destiny is surging, whirling them in confusion. exalting them, destroying them! Who among them sees and comprehends what is being done to them and around them? . . How superficial, how narrow, how small minded are the judgments and measures of Western Europe and America! . . . . What, indeed, does anyone know of the direction in which his very own destiny is facing? All we have is a number of absurd catchwords such as 'overcoming the economic crisis', 'mutual understanding of nations', 'national security and self-sufficiency' with which to overcome catastrophes within the space of a generation or two." (*Ibid.*, pp. 3-4.)

"There is universal dread of reality. . . . It is the spiritual weakness of decadent man of higher civilizations, who lives in his cities cut off from . . . the soil, and, thereby, from the experiencing of destiny, time, and death in nature herself. . . . He cannot bear . . . the relentless course of things . . . striding pitilessly through the centuries into which the individual with his tiny scrap of private life is inevitably born at the appointed place. This is what he longs to forget, refute, or contest. . . . Like a grotesque ostrich he buries his head in hopes. . . . The cowardice of the cities shouts its apparent optimism to the world at large from very fear. Reality is no longer to be borne. The wish picture of the future is set in place of facts, although fate has never taken any notice of human fancies, from the children's Land of the Do-Nothing to the Cuckoo World Peace and Workers' Paradise of the grown-ups." (*Ibid.*, 7-8)

"The peace period of 1870-1914, and the memory of it, rendered all white men self-satisfied, covetous, void of understanding, and incapable of bearing misfortune. We see the result in the Utopian conceptions and challenges which today form part of every demagogue's program, challenges to the age, to the State, to parties, and, in fact, to everyone else in complete disregard of possibility or of duty, doing, and foregoing." (*Ibid.*, 16-17)

"The World War [Spengler died in 1936] was but the first flash and crash from the fateful thundercloud which is passing over this century. . . . The form of the World is being remoulded at the foundations, regardless of the desire and intentions of the majority or of the number of victims demanded by every such decision. But who understands this? Who is facing it? The people in this time are diminutive. They can no longer bear tragedy, either on the stage or in real life. They crave happy endings of insipid novels, so miserable and weary are they. But the destiny which pitched them into these decades now takes them by the collar and does with them what has to be done, whether they will or no." (*Ibid.*, 18)

"We have entered upon the age of world wars. It began in the nineteenth century and will outlast the present one and probably the next. It signifies the transition from the eighteenth century world of states to the Imperium Mundi." (*Ibid.*, 24)

"In the place of direct wars between 1870 and 1914 we have the indirect variety in the form of a steady increase of war preparedness, of the pace of armament and technical invention; a war in which there are similarly victories, defeats, and short-lived peace treaties." (*Ibid.*, 48)

"It must be stated again and again that this society in which our time is . . . is sick, sick in its instincts and, therefore, in its mind. . . . It offers no defense. It takes pleasure in its own vilification and disintegration." (*Ibid.*, 118)

"The great cultures accomplish their majestic wave cycles . . . They appear suddenly, swell in splendid lines, flatten again and vanish and the face of the waters is once more a sleeping waste. A culture is born in the moment a great soul awakens out of the proto-spirituality [*dem urseelenhaften Zustande*] of our childish humanity, and detaches itself, a form, from the formless, a bounded and mortal thing from the boundless and enduring. It blooms in the soil of an exactly definable landscape, to which plant-wise it remains bound. It dies when this soul has actualized the full sum of its possibilities in the shape of peoples, languages. dogmas, arts, states, sciences, and reverts into the proto-soul. . . . Thus, the inward and outward fulfillment, the finality which awaits every living culture, is the purport of all historic "declines'. The decline of the West will occupy the first centuries of the coming millennium. It is heralded already and sensible in and around us today. Every culture passes through the age phases of the individual men. Each has its childhood, youth, manhood, and old age. . . . The notion of life duration as applied to man, an oak, a blade of grass, comprises a specific time value, which is quite independent of all the accidents of the individual case. . . . Without doubt the biology of the future will —in opposition to Darwinism and to the exclusion in principle of causal fitness, motives for the origin of the species—take these pre-ordained life durations as the starting point for a new enunciation of its problem. The duration of a generation—whatever be its nature—is a fact of almost mystical significance. . . . Such relations also are valid . . . for all the higher cultures. Every culture, every adolescence and maturing and decay of a culture, has a definite duration, always the same, always recurring with the emphasis of a symbol." (*Decline of the West,* 60-66)

Such is a fair summary of Spengler. In spite of his errors of determinism, of equating society to a biological organism, of underestimating the unique resiliency and creativity of the West, and his cold, fish-blooded tendency to observe the decay rather than also understand its alternative, Spengler is a giant in his time, a man of prophetic insight. He was the first great writer of international reputation to dare to tell the West bluntly in non-fiction that it is in decline. His courage and prophetic insight dared to tell the Nazis in 1934 in his Fatherland that they were bearing his nation into a destiny he feared for all the West, not only Germany. Despising the decadence of Germany after the first World War, he also mistrusted the Nazis and frankly told them in his *Hour of Decision* that they would be judged for their crimes on the altars of history. This great man foresaw clearly half of his time, the decline of the West, the tyranny and Caesarism of the future, the struggle for the Imperium Mundi. In his sad pessimism and in his animosity to Christianity, both of which he inherited from Nietzsche, Spengler was unfortunately denied the light to perceive that the decline which he so well understood was also a transition to a new spiritual form of Western civilization. Modernity, doubtless, owes much to Spengler. His, however, is only a Teutonic voice of defiance and despair amid our decay. Bravely, unflinchingly he marches into the Twilight of the Gods. He is one of the best of modern pagans. This book, the author hopes, may counteract the paganism and hopelessness of Spengler and do more good. His paganism and pessimism are the reasons for his limitations. The half of the future he foresaw is true. The half he did not see is the more important and creative half.

The revolt of the masses

Part of this future has already been seen by the great

contemporary Spanish philosopher, Ortega y Gasset. This book, although owing nothing consciously to him, will occasionally skirt some of his basic ideas, interpreting them with entirely different emphasis. Like Spengler, Ortega y Gasset shares in some of the almost inescapable marks of his race, milieu, and time. The great French philosopher and literary critic, Taine, was wrong when he believed that these forces completely determine an author. He was right when he stressed their importance. Free will can overcome the race, the environment, and the time. Otherwise, man would remain a helpless puppet of the currents of his age, a victim of purely physical forces beyond his control. But free will does not completely obliterate the trace of such forces and many do not use their free will to overcome them. It was comparatively easy for Spengler to escape the scourge of materialistic "liberalism" which scars Ortega y Gasset. Intellectual Germans have been less tainted with it than the intellectuals of other lands. It was more difficult for a Romance intellectual to escape being a materialistic "liberal", and, unfortunately, Ortega y Gasset did not well succeed. Ortega sees in our time chiefly one phase of our future transition; it is the negative phase of convulsion and chaos rather than a creative phase of the future. He understands our time as a revolt of the masses. As a materialistic "liberal" and, therefore, reactionary sensatist, he does not see that it will lead to the inevitable chaos and destruction of the modern sensate world to whose values he clings. Spengler understood the revolt from beneath very clearly in its end result, the destruction of sensate standards of creativity. But he suggested only the pagan alternative—crushing the masses.

Seen from a broader viewpoint than either Spengler

or Ortega y Gasset possessed, the revolt of the masses belongs both to the decline of the sensate world and the rise of the spiritual one. In their *negative* aspects the masses of common people of the West are often greedy and savagely materialistic.

But in their greed and materialism they are often more sinned against than sinning; they are really thirsting for justice in their own inadequate way. Living in the midst of a world where the emphasis has been fairly constantly on the getting and having and enjoying, they have demanded that the materialistic overtone of society become universally operative and effective and that everybody get and have and enjoy, not only a privileged few. And if their greed and materialism often seem savage and ugly, it needs to be said in favor of those having little that it is not easy to avoid violent jealousy and savageness when many around them have so much and they so little. It is easy to be less savage when one is sated than when one is hungry.

The dispossessed do not reason in their poverty. Still less do they bring a Christian approach to it. They simply see that some have terribly much and they terribly little. They demand that the sensate society function and that they who have not begin to have. They do not reason that their demands sometimes can upset the whole sensate order, that many prizes of the sensate society are rare and accessible to only a few. Superlativeness, uniqueness are qualities of the highest ranges in a sensate society as elsewhere. The dispossessed have no tradition of loyalty to superlativeness. They are simply demanding what is to them sensate justice—the same having and getting and enjoying which everyone else has. They are not interested in political and social theories about equal opportunity. They only want the theories to work. They are not interested in the pursuit of sensate happiness guaranteed to them by their various governments. They want the happiness manifest, right here and now, today. Pursuit unless it ends in attainment is mere activity for activity's sake. They refuse to be barred from happiness by mere accidents of birth or temperament or talent. They are also shrewd enough to know that these are mere accidents and also perspicacious enough to see that not all of those who have have any special talents or abilities which guaranteed their having and which separate them as the elect from the dispossessed. The emphasis is on getting and having and enjoying—and they mean to get and have and enjoy. And if the *beati possidentes* try to dissuade them by arguments of birth or inheritance or talent or genius or temperament, they will retort that these are mere accidents and they will begin to manoeuver the accidents to suit themselves.

The French Revolution was the first great historical upsurge of the dispossessed elements in modern times, and it has really never ended, nor will it end for generations to come. The negative forces which motivate the revolt of the dispossessed elements are principally greed and hate. They want what others have and what they have not had an opportunity—and often the ambition—to get. They are determined to get, and get they will. What they do not get through the intrigues of demagogues they will take through force. In this they will frequently be pure elements of destruction. Often stronger than their passions for getting, however, is their hate. They hate the world of wealth and prestige and comfort which is beyond them. They also fear it and often their fear has historically perfectly just foundations. Fear will drive man to any extremes and the fear and juxtaposition of what he feels to be superior can drive him to bestial savagery. He hates his superiors and would like to destroy them, not only enviously because the juxtaposition wounds his vanity, but quite honestly because it frightens him. The fear inspired by superiority cannot be reasoned away. Therefore, the under elements to put an end to their fear would like to eliminate the physical and tangible causes of it, all those persons and institutions and ideals which they sense to be above them. The revolt from under is determined to destroy what is above it. It cloaks its materialism and its greed and its hate with liberal shibboleths of liberty and equality. But it is the liberty and equality of the mob, and as such it is fatal to the standards of a sensate culture. In the more savage phases of the decline of our time it will attack all heads which rise above its own and literally or figuratively cut them off to make their bearers equal. The cry of the French Revolution, it needs be remembered, was not threefold but fourfold: liberty, equality, fraternity, *or* death; death for all those who did not accept the criteria of the mob. One of the "judges" of the French Revolution expressed it concisely and succinctly: "If these damned aristocrats will not be our equals, then we shall make them a head shorter." The greed and hate of the masses, misled and wronged as they frequently will be, will potentially make the future generations an unbelievable inferno of savagery, a French Revolution on an international scale, continuing for irregular intervals for generations, even centuries. There undoubtedly will be occasional recurrences and intermittent continuations of it as there already have been since 1789.

However, it is more probable that throughout much of our transition into the world of the spirit the revolt of the masses will assume a less violent form, although one which will just as effectively overthrow the sensate world as violent revolutions. Decadent Western society will make progressively greater materialistic concessions to the masses to hold them in check as it has already begun frequently to do. Demagogues will lead them by the nose and keep them, at least, partly stultified by *panem et circenses, Kraft durch Freude,* "progressive", liberalistic innovations, with beer for all, even champagne for the more loyal party members. Emphasis will be on mass production, on quantity rather than quality. The standards and criteria of the sensate society will plummet rapidly in the scramble to feed and house and clothe the millions. It will be a difficult world for those with Epicurean and aristocratic sensate tastes. Selectivity in food, discrimination in its taste and preparation, will yield to the technique of production and preparation *en masse.* Taste in dress and home appointments will decline. "Antiques" of an earlier, more creative sensate period may remain as the only source of creative individualism for the few who may try to maintain high sensate standards in home furnishings and decoration during the decline. Even the homes themselves will probably be standardized by mass production and the passion for gadgetized efficiency. Mass-designed and factory-made along lines of decadent sensatism they will figuratively make an architect of the more creative sensate period like Christopher Wren roll in agony in his grave. The architect and the engineer "trained" *en masse* in the decadent technical schools will replace the sensitive designer of the more creative sensate era. The dullards and "experts" will be impressed by the speed and rapidity and efficiency of all this strangulation of creative individualism and will call it "progress". Capitalism will cooperate in the decline under mass production, sensing a last opportunity to still the savage jealousy of the mob by flattering its lower taste for inferior things and objects and possessions of decadent sensate standards.

Standards not only of taste but of morality also will decline under the impact of vulgarity brought about by the revolt of the masses especially to the degree that these are robbed of the last vestiges of religion by the pagan influence and programs and emphases of the demagogue leaders. Chafing under restraint and discipline they will upset what remnants of the moral law may yet remain untrampled by the bad example of the "upper classes". The millions will not observe even the hypocrisies and shams and attempts at concealment which sometimes motivate the upper classes in their moral decadence. Disciplines and restraints of every sort will be frowned upon and a nihilism of vulgarity will prevail. Nihilism is the expression of the abysmal hatred felt by the under elements against higher sensate form of every sort. In a more creative sensate period all classes have a certain tact, a certain sense for tradition, an admission that there should be standards and ideals upheld by the inheritance of all men of good will. In our sensate decline our age has become vulgar, and most people already have no idea to what extent they themselves are tainted. The bad manners of all classes, the general tendency to connive at a transaction, no matter how shady, if it promises to bring in money, the unashamed debauchery of politics, the debauchery of music and the dance by the importations from the African jungle, the debauchery of education, the debauchery of literature in its *recherche* of the lurid or shocking, the efforts of writers to win popularity by ridiculing in their books the correct, the bad taste shown equally by the upper classes in throwing off sound restraint and tradition, are evidence that it is a vulgar revolt against civilization which already begins to give the tone.

The under elements are beginning to unchain the hatred which burns to destroy. There is envy or hate of everything which is not available to all, and there is an undercurrent of resentment muttering that everything must be levelled. Not only tradition, refinement, but every kind of sensate grace, beauty, taste, good manners, elegance, self-discipline irritate the vulgar soul till its blood boils. The preference for Homer to a boxing-match, for Beethoven to a football game, for Brahms to boogie-woogie, the appreciation of fine art and music and poetry, even the sensate delight in a well kept garden of trees or flowers or fruits, all this is to be smashed, stamped out, communized. Culture because of its superiority is the enemy of the masses. Because it is beyond the mass, it must be stamped out or prostituted to that level where even the most lowly can "assimilate" it.

The emphasis upon quantity over quality, the hostility to taste and tradition, the rejection or prostitution of culture in the revolt of the masses, will overthrow the sensate culture just as inevitably as the recurrence of violent revolution after revolution, war upon war. The gradual upheaval differs only in the degree of the severity of the convulsion. It does not differ an iota in the final goal and end result.

Seen from a broader view than from the sympathetic approval of Ortega y Gasset or the will to crush of Spengler, the revolt of the masses has been inevitable from the stage our sensate culture reached in the late eighteenth century, and its end result, namely, the death of the sensate society, can be turned either to good or to evil according to the way which the free will of man himself determines. A sensate culture bears within itself the seeds of its own decay. Since the values of such a culture are based upon the getting and having and enjoying, all, or almost all, its members must get and have and enjoy, and equally so. It is not just that some should get and have and enjoy so much and others be deprived even of necessities. If such a situation exists, and it unquestionably does, the sensate society contradicts its own tests of value to become illogical. If the tests of value are in the getting, the having, and the enjoying, then all should get and have and enjoy equally. Yet, this too contradicts human nature and is illogical. Individuals differ in their ability to get and have and enjoy. What some require years in getting, or never get, others acquire in a trice. What some might enjoy for a decade, others fling away in a single orgy. Over the decades and centuries of a sensate culture wide chasms open between the amounts which the individual members are able to get, to have, and to enjoy. At its decay the sensate society tends to divide itself into the haves and the have-nots. The divisions and distinctions between these groups may be, in effect, quite tenuous. But envy and suspicion and greed make them very real. During the earlier, creative period of a sensate society it is realized that not much is required to make a sensate family "happy". A small, well-preserved homestead will suffice, or a worthy and needful craft honestly and reputably practised, a tiny plot of land bearing evidence of cultivation by affectionate or ambitious hands, a miner's spotless home, a few good books. It is not a question of how much one has but what one has and the way in which one has it. Mere having and the quantity of having do not vulgarize a sensate period during its years of creativity. Philemon and Baucis can be as contented as Croesus, or more so.

After the critical period of a sensate culture sets in, quantity becomes important. It affects all classes. In the scramble to get many acquire very little or close to nothing at all. Those who do get are not satisfied and want more. The sensate cravings of man to possess and enjoy grow by feeding and overreach themselves so that he cannot be sated. By the end of the eighteenth century those who were beginning to have little had this fact shouted to their attention. The age of pamphlets and of journalism began. The propaganda of the French *philosophes* of the eighteenth century and of the British, American, French, German, Italian, and Russian "liberals" of the nineteenth century fanned the desires of the have-nots and fed the revolt from below. Sensate society became divided by hate and jealousy, and the decay, begun first slowly, moves now at an ever accelerating speed. A sensate world in which some have so much and others so little is impossible. It is morally wrong by sensate standards; for having and enjoying are the tests of value. The revolt of the masses was, thus, necessary, inevitable. They were, however, inflamed by the propaganda of the journalists and the demagogues more than was needful. They sometimes had enough to be sensately creative, at least at the height of the sensate period. But there is at no period enough to go around so that everyone may have everything; and that is, in the long run, all that will satisfy the boundless cravings of the masses of sensate man.

And yet, the revolt of the masses has other than negative aspects. It is a true part of the transition into a better world. If it is a revolt from under, there should in a Christian world really be no clear cut under. Our world is struggling toward a Christian basis again. To accomplish this goal, there must be a new social order evolved, where the stress is not on top and middle and under, but on the common brotherhood of man under God. Muddled and confused and ugly as the tempest may be, it is perhaps necessary in order that a better world may be born. For in the best sense it is injustice that is being assaulted in our time by the revolt of the masses.

For some to have so much and others so little is unjust not only by sensate standards. It is unjust equally by Christian ones. God made His gifts for all, to be shared in by all His children. He did not make them just for rich white people and decree that His yellow and black and brown and red and under middle class white children should be dispossessed. The dispossessed exist because men have ignored God's laws and the spirit of God's laws. The dispossessed in a certain limited sense are reestablishing God's laws and God's justice when they ask their share in His gifts.

One of the great tragedies of our Renaissance is that the dispossessed have so little insight into the non-materialistic emphasis of Christianity in their asking. The bourgeois world in rejecting Christianity for itself made it also very difficult for the poor, who ought to be the best Christians, for they have God's very special Love and blessing. But the bourgeois have caused that Love and blessing to sour among the poor and dispossessed into envy and hate. Yet, the tragedy of our Renaissance in this respect is not hopeless. The laboring and dispossessed classes of the world number countless millions who recognize Peter's throne. The social teaching of the Church can readily be the leaven which will render the social upheaval of our Renaissance God's way of getting rid of the injustices of the old outmoded sensate world of the past.

Popes Leo XIII and Pius XI and the present Pope have attempted a just compromise between the masses and the capitalists. Their encyclicals set up adequate standards of social justice for both parties and have been the outstanding Christian and moral principles enunciated to halt the cleavage in the social order and the threat of chaos from below. They do very much to mitigate the savageness of the conflict and call the attention of both employer and employee to their mutual and interdependent bonds of duty and justice, restraint and discipline by which to maintain the social order. The period of greatest efficacy for these encyclicals may, however, be admittedly generations in the future. They are part of the transition into the civilization of the spirit and probably will not be able to exert their full affect in some aspects of the decadence of the sensate world. The demagogues and politicians will promise the masses more and more materialistically in order to enjoy the power of elected office over them. They will not dare to call attention to the bonds of duty and restraint, of discipline and unselfishness emphasized in the papal encyclicals. The demagogues themselves will frequently be Marxians and anticlericals. The very name of Rome will be anathema to them. Likewise, the unfortunate division in Christianity which struck Europe at the beginning of its sensate period will render them suspect to thousands of employers and millions of employees who out of ingrained prejudice, ignorance, and suspicion will not see in the encyclicals their potential excellence. The revolt of the masses threatens to continue apace as it did in Rome until it upheaves the whole sensate order. Quality, which is the very essence of a high sensate order, will decline. Quantity will prevail over it for a time so that all may have their bread and circuses. And, finally, as capitalism will be overthrown, the figurative goose that layed the golden egg will have disappeared and even quantity will be exhausted, and once more universal misery and poverty will prevail as it did at the disintegration of Rome. Socialism which begins with everyone's having something explodes into chaos with no one's having anything except the incubus bureaucrats. Without values of things anywhere to turn to, man by the sheer shock of physical reality in quest of values can be forced to create for himself new values of the spirit.

Or as a more rational alternative we can build a new brotherhood of man using, for example, the papal encyclicals as a foundation stone of the social order. The encyclicals emphasize the right of private property. They acknowledge that capital is entitled to a just return for its investment. But equally they stress that property rights must not take precedence over human rights. They stress that all men have an obligation to contribute to the common good and promote the common good, that it is inherent in the Christian law that neither group, either capital or labor, can ride rough-shod over the other without upsetting the social order. The encyclicals have been called socialistic. But such an accusation is slanderous nonsense indicating ignorance of both socialism and the encyclicals. Their emphasis is not materialistically rooted as is that of socialism. They deal with the material order only as a means to an end. They attempt to establish harmony in the material order so that man may live in tranquility and peace so as more adequately to love and know and serve God. The encyclicals on labor and capital contain some of the profoundest teaching of the Church with regard to the terrestrial order. The choice between chaos from below and order in our time depends to no small degree to what extent both capital and labor are willing to implement the principles of the encyclicals into action. Historically, capitalism in its development has been far enough away from the Christian non-materialistic emphasis to make it dubious that such implementation will come spontaneously from capitalism. In more recent years the materialism of capital has been re-mirrored fourfold in labor because in the latter it is essentially an unsated and, therefore, more violent materialism.

The capitalists in our day are playing a rôle very similar to that of the humanists in education. The world of both seems doomed for foreseeable time. Both represented some of the creative best in the sensate world. Their decline is synchronized and, as they fall, the world in which they represented certain aspects of the best part of their culture tumbles with them into impotency and vulgarity. Capitalism was the spirit behind much of the creative and productive genius of the sensate world just as humanism was the spirit behind its intellectual genius. Just as humanism, with its emphasis upon the needs and nature of man, bore within itself the seeds of its own destruction and fell into the trivia and minutiae of immediacy, so capitalism bore within itself the seeds of its own destruction. Its crass materialism and competitive spirit has spread almost universal greed among all classes of men. It is only reaping the whirlwind of evil greed which it has sowed. Furthermore, capitalism rested upon the supposition that for the boy of brains and perseverance and ability, regardless of birth or rank or extraction, there was always boundless opportunity. But this was true only at the creative level of the sensate culture. Capitalism came to freeze itself into a more rigid system than the royalty it had dispossessed. Inheritance and influence came to be as important as merit, and eventually more important. Men of intelligence and perseverance and ability became enmeshed in the cogs of capitalism and could not hope for recognition. They knew they were as able as, and often abler than, those who had succeeded. Since capitalism became false to its promise of boundless opportunity for the able, the able became often false to it. Embittered and frustrated, they turned against capitalism and as *déclassés* joined the revolt of the masses, becoming the pamphleteers, the journalists, the traitors to class, the politicians, the demagogues of the under elements. Unable to deal in thousands and millions of dollars, they deal with thousands or millions of votes and are often the real forces behind the revolt and the savage upsurge of the masses.

Now, in the long run, this upsurge of the masses and the eventual chaos which it will evoke in the sensate order may very well redound to the good of Western humanity and be much more positive than negative. As a minimum it will help the future world of the spirit into being by the very ruin of the decadent sensate civilization if that is the only way the future can be born of a dull, uncomprehending West. Christ consistently stressed that the things of this world cannot be prime tests of values. This holds for the rich, the poor, and the middle classes. If man is so blind in our time that he can learn this truth only by having his earth-earthy values taken from him, even the most chaotic destruction from the revolt of the masses is a positive gain toward the reestablishment of true values. The modern decadent division of the West into the haves and have-nots, whether real or fancied, is impossible as a permanent order: "A house divided against itself cannot long endure." A healthy, creative social order cannot be sundered by a hostile division of classes. This fact will be the long range lesson of the revolt of the masses. In the future society of the spirit classes may be inevitable. Man is not equal, either biologically or physically, and still less so temperamentally and spiritually. All the man-made laws of liberty, equality, fraternity, or death, which may be passed in the coming years of decadence, cannot undo the God-given individual differences in ability and talent, insight and inspiration and imagination which have their expression in various classes. Equality cannot be effectively legislated and all attempts to do so may eventuate as futile and ridiculous. But the inequality of man should never be used in terms of the suppression and cruelty of man against man. Men will have learned from the awful chaos and conflicts of the upheaval that mutual obligations, mutual duties bind all responsible men. Responsibility of class to class and man to man will be one of the healthy signs of the rise of the future spiritual society. Then, the encyclicals of our great transition popes will have more fruitful soil in which to be effective. In a spiritual society the stress will no longer be on the getting, the having, the enjoying. There will be once more opportunity for stress of duty and responsibility for justice and right not only as ends in themselves but, more important yet, as means for the honor and service and love of God. Seen thus in long range, the revolt of the masses, which will be one of the most characteristic movements of the twentieth century, will neither be *per se* a good as Ortega y Gasset observes it, nor an evil as Spengler understands it. It will be a force for either good or evil according as the free will of man will make it. In the long run it may be most creative in building the world of the spirit.

Dostoievski, torch-bearer of the future

Through Gethsemane and Calvary the modern world may need to go to find the way again to Christ. Sorrow, misery, despoilment, dispossession, revolution, upheaval, chaos frighten the mind and heart and soul of man—and with much reason. But the goal and end—the reunion of man with God—are after all the most important aspects of our time. We must get back to God. Nothing else really matters. The difficulties through which we may have to go can be a real purgatory. But if they help us into the Kingdom of God, far from being in vain, they will have really been necessary. Human suffering from a Christian standpoint is a privilege. It makes men partakers with Christ in the atonement for the monstrous evil of sin, the monstrous rebellion of the creature against his Creator, the monstrous preferment of evil to the perfection of God. Out of suffering the new world may need to be born. *Per aspera ad Christum.* Belloc, Claudel, Péguy, Dawson, Chesterton and many others have in part glimpsed this aspect of our struggle back to God, have seen some groping vision of the moulding of the new world. But one man has seen it better than any modern to date, and he was the first and greatest of the modern authors to see it and summarize it somewhat succinctly, to tell the modern world that it was an age of rotting materialism and that it must get back to its Redeemer. This was the message of Dostoievski.

Dostoievski has been the closest to a seer of any great author the modern world has had. In his day, outside of the Popes and saints and the expected workers in the vineyard of the Lord, Dostoievski was terribly alone. Yet, he was confident of the triumph and righteousness of the new awakening spirit. He realized that out of its pitiful despair and blind groping chaos the world will be born anew.

It was terribly important for a layman to say this in Dostoievski's time. Dostoievski admittedly did not always see and act as well in the crisis-facing of our time as Church and saints and Popes have done. But that is the perennial province of Church and Popes and saints to see and teach and preach the wonder of God. Men would be astounded if they did not. But what was terribly needed at the middle of the nineteenth century was that some one outside the obvious vineyard of the Lord should raise his voice throughout Europe and tell his continent of its disease. The voice of the Church, of the Popes, of the saints was suspect to many. Prejudice, blindness, ignorance both wilful and semi-wilful, closed the minds of many. But a layman seer's voice was not suspect. He had no axe to grind. There was great need for such a voice to ring clear and tell the world to come back to God.

Dostoievski was a great visionary, Europe's foremost modern genius and Russia's greatest gift to thought and letters, and, perhaps, Russia's greatest gift to Christianity. His work does much to compensate for the generally reactionary rôle which Russia seems certain to play in our New Renaissance. It is interesting that he and Berdyayev and Sorokin, who so adequately in various aspects

understand our time, all come from that country which
of all the lands of the West—if Russia is indeed of the
West at all—most reactionarily puts its faith most thoroughly in Marxian materialism, in outmoded science, in
machines and power, come from Russia always centuries
behind the times and especially so now with its faith in the
disintegrating props of a dissolving world. Men like Dostoievski, Berdyayev, Sorokin do much to overbalance the
reaction and blindness of a whole nation of Ehrenburgs,
Gorkis, Sholokhovs, Lenins, Trotskys, Bakunins, Kropot-
kins, Kalinins, and Alexander Blocks.

Dostoievski speaks with the voice of the mystery of
Russia and the voice of the mystery of the world, a voice
which they have tried to force into utter silence in Russia,
down it with the clang of machines and the roar of engines, trying to make men's souls into machines. Yet,
Dostoievski is a deeply Russian author and his work is
a Russian Christian interpretation of the Universal. To
understand Dostoievski integrally is to assimilate an essential part of the mystery of Russia and the meaning of our
time. Such a discovery brings the richest of rewards. It
puts one in harmony with the most important current of
our time, gives one vision into the dawning world. The
Church, the New Testament, St. Thomas Aquinas, and
Dostoievski are the stuff out of which are springing the
spirit of the new world, the Love of God and His Divine
Son. They are the voices crying to man to realize his own
insufficiency and error, to come back to God.

With Dostoievski, a new soul and a clearer perception
of the world became possible in our day. He was the
herald of the spirit of the new world on its way to ac-
complishment. His art was prophetic, tackling the world
in the process of becoming. Because he broke with the

dying past, his work does not deal with man in his stable surroundings, the normal and rational forms of everyday social life. He deals with man as he finds man at his crisis, he deals with him in his wickedness, his unconsciousness, his folly. But at the same time he points him to his future —in Christ. In Christ, Dostoievski saw the only hope for man out of his darkness and this significantly at the same time when so many of the great writers of the West, Whitman, Twain, Marx, Renan, Maupassant, Leconte de Lisle, Zola, for example, were doing all in their power to increase the darkness and hopelessness. Because Dostoievski dealt with the wickedness of man, he has been variously interpreted as nothing more than another "realist". This is utterly to misundestand him. He deals with the sick man only to emphasize the cure—Christ.

He and Zola, for example, are at utterly opposite poles. Zola and the typical realist deal with disease *per se*. They analyze and describe the diseases of man, bury their fingers in the sores of mankind, threaten us all with pestilence. Theirs is the laboratory method, that of analysis and examination, as much as such processes can be transferred to literature. In those rare instances where they suggest the cure, it is only some social or economic or scientific palliative which when tried spreads the evil they fancied it might cure.

For Dostoievski on the other hand the cure is everything; and there is only one cure possible, Christ, the God-Man, the Son of God. When he probes into the disease and suffering of man, it is only to point out that this disease and suffering is real, that it must be recognized and then confessed, so repentance can be made. He understood so well that the sinner must first recognize his sin, confess it. The *peccavi* and *confiteor* are necessary first steps before man can understand the full import of "Come unto me all ye who are heavily burdened and I will refresh you". Therefore, he probes human nature not in sanity but in insanity, not in law abidingness but in criminality. He concentrates on men, our so frequent modern men, who have been torn from their divine origins and been immersed in the stench and beastliness of our modern decadent cities where their lives and their world revolve around the values of the machine rather than the values of the soul. Petersburg in particular he saw as such a city, Petersburg begotten by erring and apostate men, Petersburg founded on the blood and the starvation and misery of the thousands of subject Ukrainians whom Pyotr Velikii had crushed and killed in its building. The whole atmosphere of this city, its lodging houses, its dirty, smelly shops he meant to be symbols of the tragedy of men who have strayed from God and fallen into this evil, reeking morass. When modern sensate man repudiated God, he cast himself into the purgatory of the industrial, mechanical city, and there he festers in expiation of his sin.

This emphasis imprints upon his work its dionysiac character which has made its comprehension so difficult for many who understand only a part of him. Accordingly, he is to some a champion of the oppressed. This he is truly like Bruce Marshall and Péguy and all the rest who work and write for the dawning world of the spirit. He realized that "What you do for the least of these, my brethren, you do to Me also." For Dostoievski human personality is inalienable and he finds it, as any spiritual person must do, equally in the most degraded specimens of mankind. The mark of God is upon the soul of the sinner as it is upon that of the just man. For others he is a ruthless genius. This too he is, ruthless against the evil and sickness of the world, quite the opposite of Tolstoi, whose doctrine, like Gandhi's, was the non-resistance to evil, *neprotiblenie zlu*. For yet others he is the prophet of a revived Eastern Christianity, the representative of Russian Orthodoxy, the predictor and foe of communism, the herald of the Russian Messianic idea. This too is all true in an awkward analytic way. But he is principally the synthesis of all these things and much more. He is the first great revolutionary spirit who stands out against stagnation and decadence. Seemingly only Berdyayev among the great critics of Dostoievski has understood this:

> "[Dostoievski's] Dionisism gives birth to tragedy, for it shows us man's nature only in a state of exaltation and after such pictures everything seems savorless and flat; it is like coming back to our own three dimensional world after visiting another and different universe. A careful reading of Dostoievski is an event in life from which the soul receives a baptism of fire. The man who has lived for a time in Dostoievski's world has seen, as it were, 'unpublished forms' of being, for he is above all a great revolutionary of the spirit opposing himself to every kind of stagnation and hardening".[1]

There is something very Christ-like in this attitude of Dostoievski's. That is precisely one of the things which Christ did in His divine mission for the salvation of mankind—oppose himself to the stagnation and hardening of the sensate world of His day.

Dostoievski ceases to be a humanitarian on the old sensate pattern, no longer having anything in common with Dickens, Emerson, or Bielinsky. While he still loves and pities mankind, he understands the significance of the Cross of Calvary. It is a spiritual love which calls man to the foot of that Cross. How different is he from Hugo or Rousseau who would make God out of the human race or some vague international state. Man in Dostoievski for the first time in a great author since Dante is no longer treated as a superficial creature but is followed in his spiritual depths. There is little reminiscent in Dostoievski of the whole unbroken line of great sensate authors who have written since the previous Renaissance. He is rather in the throes of religious anguish. He seeks salvation, he thirsts to make expiation and help others make expiation. He suffers for the world and wants to help the world. In this respect he is very much like Dante. There is a liberation of the spirit in him, a joy, as there is in Dante, because he knows the way of suffering, the way of Gethsemane, the way of the Cross, the way to Calvary. It is the path that the Christian has to tread. Dostoievski renewed the faith in the depths of man which had not been recognized since the last Renaissance except by the occasional religious writers so unrepresentative of their civilization's dominant tones, St. Thomas à Kempis, François de Sales, Bossuet. Dostoievski knew how humanism and science can destroy the deeper man, how he can be born again only through God. Of them he wrote: "No other expression of atheism has ever had such a force in Europe." Out of this insight he gave up the humanistic and humanitarian idea of man so prevalent among his better European contemporaries and believed in man the Christian way, in man whose path of salvation leads to Christ. For that reason even in treating of the most sinful men such as murderers (Raskalnikov), adulterers (the Karamazovwi), Dostoievski is never a pessimistic or despairing writer. There is always light in his darkness; and it is the light of Christ.

Berdyayev expresses this anti-humanistic side of Dostoievski most understandingly:

"When the humanist era was established, with its self-affirmation and shutting up of man within the walls of nature, Heaven and Hell were closed—but an infinity of worlds was opened. . . . Man was lost in these vast solitudes which were no longer subject to any cosmic order. So he turned inward to himself, entering the psychic realm, and took refuge more and more in the earth, frightened of being separated from her in the face of this new and strange infinitude. . . . During the course of the modern period man had tried to confine himself to the surface of the earth and to enclose himself within a purely human universe. God and Satan, Heaven and Hell were definitely relegated to the regions of the unknowable, as having no communication with the world, until at length they were deprived of all reality. Man himself became a flat creature in two dimensions —he had lost that of depth. His soul was left to him, but his spirit had gone. But the time came when the creative and joyous energy that marked the Renaissance dried up, and man began to feel that the earth was not so solid under his feet as he had thought. Sudden rumblings were heard and the volcanic nature of the underworld was manifested. In man himself an abyss opened and therein God and Heaven, the Devil and Hell were revealed anew. At first one could only grope about in these depths, for the daylight of the world of the soul and of her material earth was fading and the abrupt kindling of a new light had not yet taken place."[2]

Because Dostoievski was the first great modern author in our New Renaissance to help kindle that light again, he will probably always be remembered in the Christian world as the torch bearer for the future. He denounced the essential defect of humanism, its powerlessness to find a solution to human destiny.

He understood that society can never be rationalized as the humanists would have it, because there is an irrational principle in it. Human nature cannot be set within the tight compartments of the eighteenth century *philosophes* and their descendants, the political prestidigitators and agitators, from Condorcet and Robespierre on to Mussolini, Roosevelt, Lenin, and Hitler. The methods to apply to man are not those of lower mathematics, for man's destiny does not depend upon such elementary trifles as the fact that two and two make four. There is always

PER ASPERA AD CHRISTUM

an irrational something left over. Mankind is not a nest
of ants arranged for the politicians' and the sociologists'
schemes. The individualistic principle will tolerate neither
the yoke of mechanistic reason nor the obligatory enslave-
ment to mass.

By this insight Dostoievski speaks out of his profound
antagonism to socialism and other forms of totalitarianism, that antagonism which is so universal among the
writers and thinkers who work for the new world of the
spirit. He rejects the earthly totalitarian Utopia as a pri-
son of the soul, a rejection developed to the utmost in the
Possessed and the *Brothers Karamazov*. Man must not
permit himself to be turned into a machine. For man is
not himself unless he is the image and likeness of God.
When he deifies himself in the socialistic state, he ceases
to be man and his own image perishes. In man's deification
in the totalitarian state Dostoievski saw the incarnation of
the Anti-Christ. The only solution to the problem he found
in Jesus Christ. Only Jesus can combat the monstrous
image of the man who wants to be God, the Superman in
action, the Anti-Christ. How clearly a full century before
its now incipient reality Dostoievski understood the modern Anti-Christ, the foul beast Rousseau and Marx unleashed!

The emphases of Dostoievski mark the beginnings of
our new age. His is the beginning of the great lay voice
to supplement the voice of the Church and the saints and
the Popes. He marks the end of the age of Galileo and of
humanism, the age of boundless faith in man unchecked by
God. His writings mark not only a crisis but the overthrow of humanism, of sensatism, of materialism as the
foundation for adequate tests of value which can appeal
to the minds of men unless they are wilfully blind. They

make it impossible for man to find final solace in the old rationalistic humanism with its self-affirmation and Emersonian self-sufficiency. Dostoievski has shown that the way to Christ lies further on, that man in the face of the challenge of the Incarnation cannot remain simply old-fashioned, sinful, self-satisfied, unrepentant man.

If Nietzsche and Spengler could only have found Dostoievski, they might have become our great modern Christian philosophers. But Nietzsche wanted to overcome man as a shame and a disgrace and he turned towards the fiction of the Superman. On the one hand, in Nietzsche, man, the last end of the humanistic cult, is found to be his own destruction by absorption into the Superman. On the other hand, in Spengler, he goes down in an irrevocable *Götterdämmerung,* an unending chaos, before the Beast man, Nihilist man, whom Rousseau unleashed. Both Nietzsche and Spengler condemn Western man to perish hopelessly one way or another. In Nietzsche man is pushed aside as something puny and disgusting, fit only to be a means to the Superman, who devours the men who grovel before him. In Spengler man is pushed aside by the Brute.

Dostoievski and those who work for the re-triumph of Christianity over the last Renaissance offer an alternative, although admitting that there may be a transition of brute, nihilistic darkness in between. With Dostoievski we modern men need to say that the religion of Jesus Christ can save man whenever he elects to use his free will to save both himself and his world. Only Christianity has cherished and protected the ideal of mankind forever, and fixed forever and forever the human image with an adequate answer in the mission of the Incarnate Son of God.

Notes to Chapter IV

1. Berdyayev, Nicholas, *Dostoievski*, p. 22, Sheed and Ward, New York (1934).
2. *Ibid.*, pp. 47-49.

CHAPTER FIVE

WHAT TO DO

The necessity of a renewal of Christianity

As DOSTOIEVSKI has so well heralded, our sensate world of the past is hopelessly inadequate and is breaking up. The disintegration and dissolution are everywhere manifest around us, in our science, our literature, our art, our education, our ethics, our morals. What does not disintegrate of its own innate rottenness is dissolved by the horrors of war and revolution which we have on a scale unprecedented before in human history. Only the most rotarian—or the most blind—of our time can guarantee that we have seen the last of the great wars. Unfortunately there seems to be overwhelming likelihood, unless man changes his entire hierarchy of values in the immediate future, that far from having had its last wars, our disintegrating world is just entering upon the age of terrible wars. If there remains enough to fight about, our wars will probably come with a haunting regularity, will, perhaps, outlast our present century and continue on well into the next. If the blindness and self-obfuscation of sensate man clinging to his decadent world endures unshaken, the wars will last until physically there will not remain enough of the sensate world in existence to be worth clinging to or fighting over. Each war will probably be worse than the preceding one, will last longer, will involve vaster and vaster areas of the world, more and more countless millions of suffering humanity in its horror and misery. Wars will prolong the agony of transition from the sensate culture to the spiritual one. They will render more chaotic and infernal the last miserable decades of sensate man. The sensate culture is too mortally stricken to be capable of preservation. It has always been too wrongly rooted, too far from truth to merit preservation. In modern times, the disease which it carries within itself is too universally disseminated within its veins, too profoundly affecting the chief areas and organs of the sensate body. The sensate world is dying; in fact, parts of it are already dead, and it is the stench of their decomposition which so nauseatingly befouls much of the atmosphere of our day. The stakes for which the sensate world is struggling are not really worth the having. What the decadents are trying to guarantee and secure is not really worth the guaranteeing and the securing. When the body is agonizing in disease beyond hope of recovery, when it makes miserable the life of the living, when its illness threatens the well being of the hale and sound seed of the future, we may consider it an act of God's mercy when he puts an end to its suffering. We should pray that in His own good time He may speed the day of our delivery. In the midst of our pest ridden culture, rather than cling to its disease, it were better for us to realize that it should perish, and as speedily as possible; else it may affect even the young life which is beginning.

So many of the values of our contemporary culture honestly do not merit being fought for. Those that are dead and that are foul with corruption should be buried. Their disappearance, far from being an evil, to be dreaded

and struggled against by the nations is a boon to humanity, a benefit, not a loss or deprivation. Those remaining
values which are not yet quite dead but which are foul
with disease and are dying are likewise not worth the
incarnadined struggle which everywhere in the twentieth
century has been raging for them. We should give tnem
their last annointing and consign them to the mercy of
God, praying that He in His infinite wisdom may as
speedily as possible release them from their death agony
and the world from their misery and poison.

With a kind of logical and ineluctable irony it seems
likely that those who will inherit the last diseased remnants of our culture in the *imperium mundi* will be the
ones least capable of supporting a healthy sensate culture.
They will lack a tradition of centuries old creative rôles
in the making of the great European sensate culture which
blossomed forth from the fourteenth through the seventeenth centuries. They will be parvenu replacement actors
who have arrived upon the stage when already the best
acts have been played. They will lack the taste and the
understanding for a great sensate culture never having
created one themselves; and they will lack the ability to
create a genuinely brilliant sensate culture, having inherited one that was already tawdry and tarnished. For it is
likely that the *imperium mundi* of the West, after the carnage and chaos of future struggles is over, will reside in
the hands of either the Soviet Union or the United States.
Both are nations begotten out of war and revolution.
Born in war and rebellion it is fitting that they should
play the leading rôles in the last awesome finale of war
and rebellion. They have both substituted for the living
creative aesthetic sensate values of the sensate culture at
its height a mechanistic and technological outlook which

places the product of the machine over and above that of the hand and mind of man. They are the last convinced worshippers at the apostate altars of the false sensate gods.

When the rest of the West has become sick unto death of machines and power and technology and arms and armies and bombs, Russia and the United States go in for greater machines and greater power and greater arms and armies and bombs. When the dawn of the New Renaissance begins to peep over the horizon for the rest of the West, Russia and the United States continue in the powers of darkness. They will struggle for the possession of a world which is already dead for what they have to offer it. They will be the great forces of reaction, of nebulous mist and tenebrous darkness, to hold back the light of the dawn. And when all the struggle is over, when the *imperium mundi* rests within the clutch either of the eagle or of the hammer and sickle, then even they who have fought and "won" will see that that for which they have struggled is not worth the having. They will have so exhausted themselves in the final carnage that they could not hold on to it, even if it were. After years of continued horror and war and misery, it will at last be realized that he who lives by the sword shall perish by it, that he who consumes the world inherits ashes. This is the prolongation of misery which hangs over the world. Only the free will of man in lifting the scales of blindness from our eyes can prevent this horror. God can help us, but it depends chiefly on our free will to prevent this prolongation of wretchedness from coming to pass.

In the face of such a break up of the world not seen in the West since the fall of Rome and on a scale of dissolution and chaos never before seen in the West, it is the most natural question in the world if men query, "What can be done?" What can be done to prevent this enduring horror and prolongation of misery from coming to pass?

It is not only fitting and proper that this question should be asked. It must be asked. And it must be asked and answered by individuals before it can be asked and answered by nations. For any action which can save our contemporary world from a prolonged chaos of horror and dissolution must be set in motion by individuals and groups of individuals. The contribution of each individual is important. He is the leaven with which the whole shall be leavened. The understanding of our crisis will not dawn to vast numbers of humanity everywhere at the same time. It will spread slowly, and each individual will have to contribute his part, do his bit in enabling another and still others to understand. The individual who understands our crisis must never permit himself to be overwhelmed by the enormity of the task which stands before him. If the individual fails to do anything about our crisis when he understands it, he is more guilty of prolonging it than those who belong to the forces of darkness and obfuscation and dullardy. Out of the understanding and the action of enough individuals, inspired with the Love of God and with the help of God, arises the hope of our salvation.

Obviously, we have already been too slow in understanding the decadence of our world to have prevented much of our misery. We may also be too slow in the future to prevent much more. What extremes we shall be able to prevent depends entirely on the degree to which individuals understand the nature and causes of our upheavals and their consequences and to what extent they move to build the new world under God. Thus, we are able to a great or small extent as we will to shorten our days of tribulation and mitigate their ravages. Our time for doing this is as long or as short as we choose to make it, depending upon how much terribleness we will to endure. If we are to put our world in order for the immediate future and that is what we should do—we have almost no time left at all. If our world is to be in order tomorrow, we must set it in order today. If on the other hand we are willing to risk one or two more wars and waste our lands in preparing for them, risk the chaos and misery of nightmares of new dread wars, we may have several decades yet in which gradually we may set our house in order. Even in this case, however, we dare not delay beyond the end of the century, and probably not even that long. If we do, the future of the spirit will be born the hard way. The sensate world will be burned to ashes until physically there will not be enough left over for sensate man to live by. Per force of brute physical necessity, he will build himself other sets of value. Having nothing left in the world except God, he will have his eyes torn open to the reality above and beyond his smouldering ruins. But in going through this apocalypse of horror man also runs some danger of becoming embittered. It will certainly not be easy for him to reconstruct an adequate world if he is despoiled of everything. Having gone through a disintegration and explosion vaster and more leveling than that which razed Rome, he will have even greater difficulty than did the survivors in Europe in the sixth and seventh and eight centuries in rebuilding a world of the spirit on the ruins of Roman civilization. That medieval man succeeded in building a great spiritual culture cannot be questioned. But what modern man should try to do is to build a better one, and for this he must not allow himself to be as blind as was Roman man. But our danger of being more blind is frighteningly great: that would render our tribulation and desolation ever so much greater. That is, modern science guarantees us an unparalleled horror in this present break down of a disintegrating world unless the free will of man chooses otherwise. Before we can get into the future, we must purge ourslves of our outmoded sensate culture. We must first go through some form of purgatory. It would be an act of wisdom and prudence as well as a source of glory to make that purgatory as short as possible by avoiding future sin and making atonement for past ones.

The answer to what we should do is extremly simple, if only the western world could understand. It is what the Church has been saying for centuries. It is simply: we must return to Christianity, we must return to Christ and live by His norms, we must build again a Christian civilization. But if simple and direct the answer is also hard for us moderns. Christianity is especially hard for sensatists. It is a light burden when once it is borne, but it looks very heavy from a distance. Christianity means putting first what sensatists put last, if, in fact, they put it at all. It means relegating to a secondary plane what they have for the last seven hundred years been promoting to the first place of importance. It means viewing as inadequate all those things and values for which the sensatists have been struggling with might and main these many centuries past.

For Christianity is first and foremost a religion which does not consider this life and what it brings with it of joy and sorrow, of happinees and suffering, an end in itself. Christianity considers this life and everything in it a preparation, a means to an end. Christianity is first and foremost a religion *sub specie aeternitatis*. The purpose of this life is to gain salvation for eternity. A life which gains that salvation, no matter how painful or materially unsuccessful it may seem, is a success. A life which loses that salvation is a failure, no matter how spectacularly happy and enriched it may seem to have been. "What matters it to a man even if he gain the whole world and lose his immortal soul? It were better for him he had never been born". If Christianity is to return to the world as its dominant source of values, it bluntly means an entire reversal of the values to which men have been clinging for seven hundred years and which have lost or are losing their validity even in an effective earthly sense. Real validity as first values they could not ever have. "And when the salt has lost its flavor, wherewith will it be salted?" For almost seven hundred years men have been holding, as Petrarca told them they should, that the things of earth and of man should come first: "It may be only glory that we seek here as long as we remain here, but that is right. Among mortals the care of things mortal should come first." Christianity at the same time that it does not deny a value to the things of earth, when they are properly received and properly used, holds that the things of God and of eternity come first. This means that all the power, the wealth, the glory, the things and possessions over which the men and nations of the earth have been so long quarreling represent a misplaced emphasis. They are never of primary importance. They may not even be of secondary importance. They may even be a downright evil, a stumbling block along the path which leads to God. Because they do represent a misplaced emphasis, the civilization which rested on them was a civilization of false and distorted values, a wrong civilization. Now that even these values have become decadent, and no longer represent even a creative paganism, the terrible distortion of the whole sensate structure appears uglier and uglier.

Yet, it will be difficult, very difficult, for men and nations to see that all the things for which they have been striving for centuries are either wrong goals or, at best, not primary ones. When we cease the mad scramble for them, the pressure on our time will be relieved. We shall come to know a new relief in the world, a new peace, such as has not existed for centuries, precisely because the causes for the upheaval in our time will have been removed. When once more we re-integrate our tests of value in accordance with the law of God, our whole society can and will fall into order. And we shall discover that the very things for which men and nations have been literally or symbolically selling their souls these many centuries past are not so important at all. Having understood this, we shall see that we can live with one another in peace again. On the replacements for the materialistic and utilitarian City of Man we can build the City of God.

This all sounds very easy until we look at the basic non-materialism of Christianity which stresses always the non-primacy of things of earth. Getting at the basic stresses of Christianity we can see how hard it is going to be for sensatists to accept it. Yet sensatists and their descendants accepted it once before. They will do so again *volentes nollentes*. But how different are the basic emphases of Christianity from those which have prevailed in the world these last seven hundred years.

> "I say to you if one strike thee on the right cheek, turn to him also the other; and if a man will contend with thee in judgment and take way thy coat, let thy cloak go also with him. . . .I say to you, love your enemies, do good to them that hate you, and pray for them that persecute you and calumniate you." Matthew, V, 39-44.
>
> "Go, sell what thou hast and give to the poor. And thou shalt have

treasure in heaven. And come follow me. . . . It is easier for a camel to pass through the eye of a needle than it is for a rich man to enter into the Kingdom of Heaven". *Ibid.*, XIX, 21-29

"Thou shalt love the Lord, thy God, with thy whole heart and with thy whole soul and with thy whole mind. . . . Thou shalt love thy neighbor as thyself." *Ibid.*, XXII, 37, 39

"Love not the world nor the things which are in the world. If any man love the world, the charity of the Father is not in him. For all that is in the world is the concupiscence of the flesh and the concupiscence of the eyes, and the pride of life, which is not of the Father." I Epistle of St. John, the Apostle, II, 15-16

"And if thy hand scandalize thee, cut it off: it is better for thee to enter into life maimed than having two hands to go into hell. . . . And if thy foot scandalize thee, cut it off. It is better for thee to enter lame into life everlasting than having two feet to be cast into the hell of unquenchable fire. . . . And if they eye scandalize thee, pluck it out. It is better for thee with one eye to enter into the Kingdom of God than having two eyes to be cast into the hell of fire." Mark, IX, 42-46

"For we brought nothing into this world: and certainly we can carry nothing out. But having food and wherewith to be covered, with these we are content. For they that will become rich fall into temptation and into the snare of the devil and into many unprofitable and hurtful desires, which drown men into destruction and into perdition. For the desire of money is the root of all evils: which some coveting have erred from the faith and have entangled themselves into many sorrows. But thou, O man of God, fly these things: and pursue justice, godliness, faith, charity, patience, mildness." I Timothy, VI, 7-12

"If any man among you seem to be wise in this world, let him become a fool, that he may be wise. For the wisdom of this world is foolishness with God. . . . Let no man, therefore, glory in men." I Corinthians III, 18-20

"Take heed and beware of all covetousness, for a man's life doth not consist in the abundance of things which he possesseth. . . . Be not solicitous for your life, what you shall eat, not for your body what you shall put on." Luke, XII, 15-33

"He that hath two coats, let him give to him that hath none; and he that hath meat let him do in like manner." *Ibid.*, III, 11

"Everyone that exalteth himself shall be humbled, and he that humbleth himself shall be exalted." *Ibid.*, XIV, 11

"Lay not up to yourselves treasures on earth where the rust and moth corrupt and where thieves break through and steal, but lay up for yourselves treasures in heaven." *Matthew* VI, 19-20

"If the world hate you, know that it hated me before you. If you had been of the world, the world would love its own; but because you are not of the world, but I have chosen you out of the world, therefore the world hateth you. . . . If they have persecuted me, they will also persecute you." John, XVI, 2

"There shall be a time when they will not endure sound doctrine but according to their own desires they will heap to themselves teachers having itching ears. And they will, indeed, turn away their hearing from the truth." II Timothy, IV, 3-4

"Know also this, that in the last days shall come dangerous times. Men shall be lovers of themselves, covetous, haughty, proud, blasphemers, ungrateful, wicked, without affection, without peace, slanderers, incontinent, unmerciful, without kindness, traitors, stubborn, puffed up and lovers of pleasures more than of God, having an appearance of godliness, but denying the power thereof. . . . But evil men and seducers shall grow worse and worse erring and driving into error." *Ibid.*, III, 1-13

"Be you humbled, therefore, under the mighty hand of God that He may exalt you in the time of visitation, casting all your care upon him, for He hath care of you." I Peter, V., 6-7

"By this shall all men know that you are my disciples, if you have love for one another." John XIII, 35

"If thy enemy be hungry, give him to eat. If he thirst give him to drink." Romans, XII, 20-21

"The Kingdom of God is not meat and drink, but justice and peace and joy and the Holy Chost." *Ibid*, XIV.. 17

"Render not evil for evil, nor railing for railing, but on the other hand render blessing. . . . Let one refrain his tongue from evil and let his lips speak no guile. . . . Let him seek after peace and pursue it." I Peter III, 10-11

That is, Christianity is a religion of Love, Love of

God and love of one's neighbor. It is a repudiation of selfishness and self-seeking. It is a religion of peace and justice and mercy. It is a religion of faith and hope. But above all it is a religion of Love, of the Love of God and of man because he is God's handiwork. It is a repudiation of materialistic values as first values. The Kingdom of its Divine Founder was not of this world, nor can the Kingdom of genuine Christians be principally of this world. Christianity is the way of life through Love and Faith and Hope to gain salvation for eternity, not to gain a million in the stock market or material security through a labor union or an old age pension in a socialistic state, although a million in the stock market or security or an old age pension in a state under God are not evil in themselves if they are accepted properly as God's gifts and used in obedience to His laws. At the same time, Christianity looks with genuine suspicion and downright distrust at worldly wealth of flesh and purse on which men set their hearts, those treasures of eye and hand in which they fire their senses. Some of these are evil in themselves and are expressly forbidden by God's Commandments. More often they are occasions to evil, gateways to wrong doing and wrong standards and values because, even if they are not always evil in themselves, they so easily enmesh and ensnare the human soul in their toils so that man is led to forget about first things. In emphasizing the non-primacy of the things of terrestrial life, Christianity emphasizes the primacy of the things of God and of eternity, the Love and knowledge and service of God, the real end of man, the enjoyment of the Beatific Vision. From the Christian viewpoint life is a preparation for eternity; it is a means to an end, rather than an end in itself. Therefore, not only are the things of earth not of primary importance but even the most tender of human relationships, those of family, are but a reflection and mirroring of a bit of that all-pervading Love of which God is the synthesis. The most perfect Christians are even urged to break their family ties and give up everything to God, that is, surrender a great good more perfectly and unreservedly to honor Him, Who is the Source of all goods. The most perfect Christians are urged to take up their Cross and follow their Divine Master without thought of the morrow. At the same time there is provided in marriage and the family an ample area of Christian living and grace and sacraments for those for whom such ascetic ways might prove too severe and who might falter before they attained their goal. All Christians are to love God, their neighbors, and their enemies, do good to all mankind, share with them of their goods, bear with them in their sorrows, in short, return good for evil. They are to abide by the things and laws of God even at the pain of death itself. Martyrdom, persecution, hate, and distrust at the hands of the world are a not improbable fate of a Christian. They were the lot of the Founder of Christianity. Even as the world hated Him, it may hate His followers, for the world knows its own and the Christian is not of this world. Suffering, that great dread of the modern pagan world, which it seeks to avoid as the root of all evil, may be the daily lot of a Christian. Suffering, far from being an evil according to the Christian standpoint, is often a special mark of God's love and favor. "Whom the Lord loveth He chastiseth." In suffering, the Christian sees an opportunity to be a co-worker with Christ making atonement in a finite way as He made atonement in an infinite way for the sins of men. Suffering on earth means also a shorter Purgatory after death. The evil that the Christian should fear is not the harm that can be done by those who have power only over the body, but rather the verdict of condemnation from Him Who has power over the soul for all eternity. Eternity—that is the end of man and the gaining of salvation in it is the real purpose of life. If salvation is won, life is a great and permanent success. If salvation is lost, life is an eternal and permanent failure. He who belongs to the forces of evil in the world, 'twere better for him had he not been born, that a mill stone had been hung about his neck and that he had been flung into the sea. All the earthly quests for power and riches and position and pleasures and enjoyments which men and nations set their hearts and minds upon are of no permanency, no primary importance, and they are frequently downright evil.

To follow the Christian way of life may seem completely mad to modern man. In some respects it certainly will not be easy, although in other respects the burdens of Christ are easy ones. For under the burdens of Christ first things are right and other difficulties can somehow be overcome or sustained. To follow the Christian way means for modern man a complete break with the past— and much of the present. It means viewing the world from an angle completely different than that from which man has been viewing the world these many hundreds of years. It means undoing much which has been done, rejecting much which has been accepted, accepting much which has been rejected, yet accepting only that which is valid, rejecting only that which is invalid. It means an entirely new and different outlook by man. It means overthrowing many of the educative and formative processes of centuries, all those wrong concepts which have driven man so far from God and rendered him so cruel and bestial, so materialistic, so bereft of Love for God and his fellow man. It means a new education, leading him to accept concepts which in his error he had thought wrong and divesting himself of ideas which in his obfuscation he had been misled to think right. It means to many in the West, especially to the Protestant world, in part a new religion. For the Protestant adjustment of the ledger six days a week to the primacy of the things of this world with a seventh day adjusted to God for the primacy of His things so He may deal handsomely by man the other six simply has no basis of fact in the emphases of the New Testament, which Protestantism in spite of its Bibliolatry has ignored. For the things of God are primary always, seven days out of seven. It means a profound and radical revolution away from the values to which the world has paid tribute, not radical in that pale sense according to which socialism or communism is radical when compared to capitalism; but radical in the sense that it gets down to the roots, the radices, of truth and says that selfishness or greed or materialism, the gospel of the primacy of the things of earth, is always wrong, no matter by what economic system it may call itself.

The ideas of Christ are as profoundly radical today as they were in 30 A. D., when they brought about His Crucifixion at the hands of the Jewish and Roman sensatists of His time. And they are just as rough on those pale decadent "radicals" of the modern sensate world, the socialists, the "liberals", the communists, as they are against any capitalist or *laissez-faire* economist. And not infrequently they are much rougher on the leftist, for his greed is often greater, his materialism much more savage, because, compared with that of the capitalist, it is unsated. Yet, the emphases of Christ are radical only in the sense that they are the roots of truth. They are not radical in the fairly common modern sense of being rabble rousing and leading to bloodshed and hatred and class division and dissension. They are revolutionary, but not revolutionary in the accepted modern sense of guillotine and purges and executioner juries and red flags and savage, anarchistic, nihilistic, atavistic bestiality. They are revolutionary in the sense of turning man around (*revolvere*) and letting him see once again where truth lies.

And hard as it may be for modern man, even downright mad as it may seem to him, the Christian way of life is the only way open to him if he is to save himself and his future civilization. In spite of all the revolutionary contradiction with his immediate past which the Christian way of life means, in spite of all the rupture which it entails with many of the educative and formative forces which made him, the Christian way of life is his only salvation. The alternatives of pragmatism, of operationalism, of expediency, of enlightened self-interest, of liberalism, of socialism, of statism, of materialism, of mechanism, of political deification of any type, we have seen all lead to the chaos of the warring jungle. Since these false panaceas of declining sensate man lack basic criteria of right and wrong, since the pragmatism and self-interest of one can be purchased at the expense of his neighbor, in the jungle of modernity his methods and truth become right who has the power to enforce them and keep them enforced on the rest of the world—and this means in our time burning the world to ashes. The activities of the statesmen, the pragmatic internationalists and nationalists, the idealists and realists, the radicals and conservatives, the ousters of wars and revolutions, the international and national quacksters of every brand in the first half of the twentieth century have been a fatal illustration of the hopelessness and shallow, despairing awfulness of all the other alternatives to Christianity.

The quacksters of our time, our presidents and führers and political prestidigitators, have been busy with everything except the values of Christianity, its supra-mundanism, its anti-materialism, its spiritual treasury, which surpasses all knowledge. Christianity has been forgotten by those who would find the answers to the problems of the world. The corner stone has been forgotten when the blind and ignorant builders of bright and better worlds have raised their structures. Scarcely any of these busy-bodies mumbled even insincere, half-hearted lip service to its values and truths and never do they get at the essence of Christianity, the Love of God. The shepherds of the people, the policy formers of modern nations, have given no chance to Christianity. Only a few writers, a few idealists like the recent Popes, scorned by the "realists" and ignored by them and excluded from the councils of the world, have raised their warning voices pointing out that with Christianity all things are possible, that without it even those measures which may sincerely be meant to help will have a devastating influence in the disintegrating system of the world. They have not been heard. Their voices have been literally voices crying in the wilderness of modern pragmatism and materialism and mechanistic internationalism. They have been drowned out by the howling of the wolves. The roaring of the Lion, the growling of the Bear, the chattering of the Eagle drown out the Lamb of Peace.

The modern proponents of pragmatic and materialistic and mechanistic alternatives to Christianity have been feverishly busy with one ramification after another of the

Hague Conference or the League of Nations or the United Nations. The "great" "modern" "scholars" and executives, leading military men and civilian chieftains with their numerically awesome supporting bureaus of advisers and experts, the "practical" economists, political scientists, sociologists, industrialists, educators, bankers, politicians, labor leaders have been terribly busy researching, and recommending an endless number of "practical" measures, concerning disarmament and armament, money and finance, tariff and free trade, currency and prices, government controls and government *laissez-faire*, international commerce and international finance. They have held meeting after meeting, session after session, on how to run the world, regulate its currency, keep its peace, enforce their will upon the nations of the earth, whether the nations of the earth wanted their will or not. They have drawn borders, shifted populations, held plebiscites, signed treaties which contradict the most elementary considerations of justice and history and decency and dignity. The best that could be said of the most honest of them is that they are sincere dullards lacking the most fundamental knowledge of the languages, the traditions, the philosophy, the history of the world areas with which they deal just as complacently as if they were bits of cardboard in a puzzle and whose inhabitants they uproot just as unfeelingly as if they were so many pigs to be carted to an abattoir. The worst that can be said of the most shameless among them is that they must knowingly be minions of Satan.

They have disarmed the vanquished, imposed their will upon them, and sworn mutual agreement and assistance to one another at the very moment they move heaven and earth to compete in military preparation against their co-signers. This materialistic pragmatic brood in the twentieth century has been having its hey-day. The results are terrible and horrible—a complete fiasco. The twentieth century has already seen the two most terrible wars and the most terrible revolutions the West has ever witnessed. The grace of God needs to become over active in Western man if he is not to be hurled into still worse wars and revolutions in the remainder of the century. For the vast military programs intended for the immediate future among the great nations prove that man fresh from war uses the armistice called "peace" to prepare for the next round of the struggle for *imperium mundi*. The shepherds of the people who have forgotten Christianity or who mumble an insincere lip service to it have not only failed to eliminate war and revolution, poverty and injustice and other calamities. They have not only failed to reduce their destructive and leveling force. They rather increase the catastrophe: they make wars more appalling and increasingly world wide, involving vaster and vaster areas and even greater millions of pitiful, suffering humanity. They brew revolutions and resentment and anger on a scale never before seen in history.

Even in our own day, when the horses of the Apocalypse ride over the earth as never before, these shepherds of the people do not try Christianity. They remain blinder and more foolish in their pseudo-practicality and their pseudo-realism, their obfuscated pagan pragmatism and power politics and their supposedly clever operationalistic schemes which simply will not work. They still talk of everything but the elementary Christian truth that any sincere and literate person could get out of a single reading of the four Gospels. They are if possible even greater

dullards than their predecessors of a generation ago because it has become increasingly clear that their pragmatism and operationalism simply lead to greater calamity.

Our shepherds of the people still plan the bright new
world on anything or everything except Christianity. It
is no wonder that for a century and a half the modern
leaders have led mankind from bad to worse. And mankind has paid, is paying, and will continue to pay for their
foolishness and its own an ever mounting price in life,
in its sacred and intimate values, in suffering and misery
and heightening tragedy until it comes to see that Christianity offers it the only way out. But with mankind as it
is and the forces leveled against Christianity being what
they are, it is not going to be an overnight's job to set the
world back into the path of Christian truth. A considerable time and increasingly severe ordeals may be inevitable
before this can be accomplished. The débris of centuries
of error and superstition in materialism and mechanism
and modernism must be cleared away. The fires which are
raging throughout the West in the twentieth century are
indicating the need of doing just that. Each successive
horror shouts louder the cry: the ways of the past have
proved wrong; the world is sick and needs to be born
anew; make straight the paths of the Lord. Christianity
is the only way out. The entire world has to be rebuilt
on Christian values. Its moral, social, intellectual, and
international order must be set in motion again. True
peace and justice and decency can be obtained only by
basing society upon Christ. This restoration cannot be
obtained by a return to the methods, the philosophies,
and the values of the outmoded sensate past. It must be
new, new with the ever pure and ever true breath of the
spirit of Christ, Who is the Way, the Truth, and the Life.

The nature of the renewal of Christianity

The first phase of the answer to the question what can be done is very simple. We must return to a Christian civilization. The second, phase, however, the return itself may be extremely difficult because it involves such a fundamental and radical change from the tests of value by which the world has been living these many centuries past.

Yet, even this second phase need not be so difficult if only the indifference and inertia and blindness of Western man can be overcome. Everything depends now on man's working in coöperation with the graces of God. This may not be so complicated as it seems. The ground work has been in the process of laying for a century or more by our poets and philosophers and Popes, Newman, Chesterton, Péguy, Thompson, Dostoievski, and all the recent Popes with their rich treasury of encyclicals on the social and political order. It remains now only for a few hundreds to follow where dozens have led. Thousands can then follow the hundreds, and millions the thousands. The time is ripe. Men everywhere long for a better order, for justice and peace and tranquility which have been brutally snatched from them in the twentieth century.

Modern men en masse may prove not to have been so blind as misled. When they hear the truth shouted at them, they may have an innate common sense and a realism that their leaders have not had. For the plain people everywhere do have a deep horror of war. And they have a realistic uneasiness that war and all its accompanying suffering impend over them. They very possibly can be made to see that the way out of war and its horrors is through a New Renaissance of Christian principles. They know instinctively as well as by fact that injustice and power politics are wrong, that they breed the whirlwinds of the future. They would be more than willing to see more adequate justice established.

The plain people, likewise, have proved they can follow Christ. When they desert Him or become indifferent to Him, their defection is largely attributable to the defection and example of their leaders. Down through history there has been a certain bed-rock of reliability among the plain people for Christ, unless they were misled or misinformed or misdirected by their leaders to further the latters' far from holy schemes. In Christ's own day many of the plain people followed Him. They were whipped into a mob against Him only by the attitudes, the example, and finally the propaganda of their leaders. In the Age of Faith the plain people followed Christ as their leaders followed Him. It is apparent they often loved Him more and understood Him better than many of their leaders. And, when, in modern times, the people fell away from Christ, the preparation for their defection had been made for centuries by their leaders. The materialistic overtones, the quest for rich and easy living so dominant today throughout the Western world, had their beginnings in the palaces of the Renaissance princes and sometimes in those of the very cardinals and Popes themselves. The plain people fell away from Christ only after they who should have served Him best had set the pace for deserting Him for the emphases of this world.

The palace of the Popes in recent centuries has done everything in its power to set in motion a trend back to Christ, a trend unmistakably followed by many of the plain people in some of the lands closest to Peter's throne.

In the tempests which divided Christendom in the sixteenth and seventeenth centuries, it was princes greedy for power and riches in this world who set the tempo for the revolt from Christ. The plain people followed more slowly and many of them did not follow the bad example of their leaders. In the shocking revolts from Christ from the French Revolution onward the tempo again was set by the leaders: first, by that part of the aristocracy in various lands which was simpering and effete and horribly ineffectual in living up to the responsibility which nobility brings with it and thus prepared the way for the whirlwind; and later set by the lawless, anarchistic, atheistic, godless preachments of the Condorcets, the Rousseau's, Robespierre's, Clootz's, Saint Simon's, Bakunin's, Lenin's, and Trotzky's. And even in those lands like France and Russia, where godless atheism for a time succeeeded in establishing its piggish reign, or in Spain or Italy or Portugal, where the forces of anti-God always lie in wait to do likewise, there always remains a great fund of devotion to Christ among the plain people. There is an ear to hear the voice and revelation of Mary in the family of a Soubirous or a Ti Marto, even when the "liberal" governments mock God. Lourdes and Fatima are proof that the superstition of modernism is never so dense among the plain people that God's light is unable to break through. Not even a third of a century of the reign of Satan has crushed the faith of the Russian plain folk any more than the tyranny of England could drive Christ and Mary from the hearts of the Irish.

Misled the folk can be, especially when the misleaders are of one's own people and race and root and language. But in our time the faith in Christ and the living by Christ and Loving Him can be re-awakened in the plain people, must be re-awakened in them, to build anew a proper world. For faith is always stronger than doubt, and love is stronger than hate. When enough of the plain people

232

have their faith in the principles of Christ re-awakened, we need not fear for the leaders. The Roman emperors who persecuted the plain Christians eighteen hundred years ago sometimes knew that the Galilean was conquering. Nor did endless centuries revolve until the emperor himself was converted to the faith of the plain people. The plain people of our time everywhere need to come to realize that we are in a New Renaissance of Christ, that the creative values of the future are the values of the spirit away from the primacy of things, of technology, of gadgets, of materialism, and mechanism.

Such a re-awakening of Christianity can probably best be made first in Ireland and Portugal, for there materialism and error and the superstition of secularism have sunk less deep root. There is less débris of false standards to be cleared away. There is probably a greater common denominator of the truth of Christ to be relied on there than elsewhere. And after them Christ seems most easily to be re-established in Spanish lands and in Italy and then in that land so pregnant a matrix of modern error— France, although there is some evidence to indicate that the Spanish lands of the New World may be ultra-reactionary, having first to go through a sensate period as the rest of the world moves in a spiritual direction. In spite of their semi-defection from God such great cultural nations as Italy and France have always maintained a bedrock of devotion to Mary and her Son upon which the foundations of the future can be built.

In the final analysis, the Romance peoples have always made relatively poor materialists. There is a spirit of *savoir vivre,* of *dolce far niente* among them which did not make them the most dangerous candidates to be world grabbers and disturbers: for after all, life is short, and why spend it rushing pell mell over the earth to lay up the vastest amounts of treasure possible? The spirit of *savoir vivre,* of *dolce far niente* by its very existence renders the Romance peoples very poor material to be too dangerous activists in the materialistic defection from God. They also have a maturity and a wisdom of the ages lacked by their Germanic and Anglo-Saxon brothers which teaches them that the things of this world are at best transitory and that there is no point in making one's self over-active in obtaining them.

Nowhere is the current of the future so unmistakably strong as it has been in the past century in the Romance lands, in the spiritual expression of France and Italy and Spain and Québec and Ibero-America, in the works and thoughts and deeds of men and women like Bernadette of Lourdes, Lucia de Fatima, Paul Claudel, Baudelaire, Charles Péguy, Sainte Thérèse of Lisieux, Maritain, François Jammes, and the recent Popes. Many of these may be only transition figures. Some of them are obviously only struggling into the future, themselves not yet all clear as to whither they are going. What Goethe in his *Faust* said of men in general applies doubly well to many figures in a Renaissance, struggling bravely but not always clearly, or consistently, into the future:

So lang er auf der Erde lebt	As long as he on earth doth live,
Es irrt der Mensch, so lang er	Man still must err, while he doth
strebt.	strive.

But the angels in heaven add:

Wer immer strebend sich bemueht	Whoever striving exerts himself
Den können wir erloesen.	Him can we redeem.

Such unclarity of struggle is greater in some like Péguy or Baudelaire than it is in others. But all represent the same aspect of the soul of the Christian future, the soul of the men of France and Italy and the Romance lands struggling out of the errors of sensatism and materialism and secularism into which they preceded the rest of the West in the thirteenth and fourteenth centuries and are now again preceding the rest of the West back into the true values of the spirit and of the future. The West needs to realize that we must get into the soul of this religious France and Italy just as those who were to play any creative rôles six hundred years ago in the past Renaissance of the senses had first to get into the spirit of these lands. France and Italy are two of the most important nations for our New Renaissance as they were for that of Petrarch and Boccaccio, Giotto and Villon.

Even if in the last desperate futile assault against God in the exploding sensate world, Bolshevism should succeed in imposing its tyranny from Hell over France and Italy, a Christian underground is assured, a new catacombs from which will arise a new born Christianity, purified and revitalized by its struggle with the forces of Satan. Bolshevism, dread horror that it is, need not strike despair in anyone for the future of Christianity. Persecution has never proved the undoing of the Church. The blood of martyrs is often to the Faith as productive as is the spring rain to the bosom of nature. Bolshevism is admittedly a nightmare of horror. But it will not for all its Asiatic reactionarism hold back the future of God. The Church abides and the gates of Hell shall not prevail against her. God cannot permanently be mocked. And if His grace is permitted by man to work only in spite of Bolshevism, then we may expect such a passion of faith in the Christian underground against it that the soldiers of the Kremlin and their minions will yield before it just as Roman legi-

235

onaries moved by the outbursts of faith of the early Christians used to ignore the orders of their chieftains and join ranks with the unarmed Christians in the arenas. They who were to persecute fell on their knees converted by the miracle of faith. God's face can shine forth even when the evil leaders of men attempt futilely to obliterate it forever. If Bolshevism can by any chance be halted from spreading its pestilence over the lands of Dante and Villon, there are already a-aborning Christian political movements in these lands which can go far in the next decade or so in re-establishing the emphases of Christ.

In the peripheral lands of Western Christianity, Scandinavia, England-Scotland, Holland, Germany and by inheritance, therefore, also the United States, the problem of the re-establishment of the principles of Christ among the plain people is essentially the same as elsewhere, although more complex. Here there is a greater faith in secularism: the superstition of modernism has deeper root. Yet, even in these lands, there is profound hunger for Christian truth. The Lutheran parts of the German world have been terribly shaken by two world wars and by the Hitlerian tyranny. The Lutheran split from central Christendom is not as independently strong as it was two short generations ago. There are also many areas of Lutheranism which remained very close in doctrine and practice to the central Christian body and eventual re-union with Rome may not prove as impossible as it seemed at the turn of the century. The fate of Lutheranism on the continent has inevitable re-echoes in Scandinavia, where already the Faith of Peter is slowly re-establishing itself after having been almost eradicated by the tyranny of persecution for well nigh four centuries. Nor should Christian emphases be particularly difficult to re-establish in Scandinavia or in Reformed Holland, for these lands never became hopelessly secularized.

The great service of Protestantism—and it may possibly be a service for which God in His infinite mercy and all-seeing wisdom can find some crumbs of pardon for those who sundered the unity of Christendom in the sixteenth and seventeenth centuries—has been to keep alive a respect for the person and many of the emphases of Christ in a world which had it not been for Protestantism might have become so completely paganized as to have lost all respect for Christ and the Bible. That Protestantism was a compromise between materialism and Christianity is indisputable. It enabled in our sensate period millions of people to hold to some fractional part of the Christian Revelation which they might have lost completely if they had had no alternative between pure Christianity and paganism. If it in its worst aspect glorified the material ledger for six days a week and in the words of such representative Protestant thinkers as John Wesley, Ben Franklin, or Cotton Mather made money making the special mark of God's favor and was thus essentially non-Christian, it on the other hand preserved respect for the name of Christ and His principles among millions of plain people who will now so much more readily be able to give heed to His gospel than they would if Christ meant nothing more to them than a memory of some mouldy, discarded figure out of a "priest-ridden" past. The fractional part of the Christian Revelation preserved in Holland, Germany, Scandinavia is vast. It can make the re-establishment—or better still the revivification—of Christian principles in these lands a comparatively easy matter; and it may take place much more quickly than will a complete reunion of Christianity in these lands with the central body of Christendom.

Perhaps in Western Christendom most difficult of all will prove the re-establishment of Christian emphases among the plain people of England and Anglo-Saxon America. Nowhere else have the superstitions of modernism and secularism and scientism taken such a firm hold. America never even had a Christian chance. The world was already rejecting Christ when it came into existence. It has never known a world with an emphasis other than materialistic. Yet, here as elsewhere the situation is far from hopeless. In spite of the centuries' ingrained commercialism, mercantilism, and profit motive outlook there is no real proof that the Anglo-Saxon is congenitally anti-Christian. The plain Anglo-Saxon respects Christianity— in theory, even if he has had little experience with it in practice. He is shocked at the disordered atheistic extremes of the Slavs and the Romance peoples. He has a great deal of innate Christian prudence and common sense which are part of the very essence of Christianity. *In extremis latet periculum*—and the Anglo-Saxon is rarely an extremist. St. Thomas Aquinas might have found him often praiseworthy. The plain Anglo-Saxon has likewise an innate hatred of tyranny and injustice and by his nature is thus very close to one of the attributes of God. He also is often very charitable to those in need: he has a feeling of responsibility to his brother man—all basic inheritances from the not too distant centuries when England was happy and merry because she was Christian.

What the Anglo-Saxon Christian, both Catholic and Protestant, will have to unlearn is the neat, compact way in which he has folded God up into a corner and told Him to stay there and mind His business, while he, the Anglo-

Saxon, concentrated on the very practical affairs of earth, dreamed the dreams of empire into reality, and flung far his trade, even among the lesser breeds without the law. Unlike the Slav and the Romance people the Anglo-Saxon in his defection from God seems scarcely capable of banishing God formally and passing laws establishing His non-existence and lopping off the heads of those who archaically and "unscientifically" invoke His name. The Anglo-Saxon would not consider it sporting or proper to snuff out the life of such non-policy forming recalcitrants.

Unfortunately, God in Anglo-Saxon lands has been for centuries so unimportant a figure in daily affairs that His non-existence really did not need to be legislated. It was *ipso facto* in their very system of mercantilism and commercialism and profit motive economics. They banished God off into a corner—and conveniently forgot about Him. They could even pull Him out in time of stress and tribulation and dust Him off as a source of strength and propaganda. Atheism and utter godlessness are scarcely the mark of the plain Anglo-Saxon. Such things are relegated to foreigners and to the comparatively rare pseudo-intellectuals of the Anglo-Saxon world who have eschewed the native common sense of their ordinary fellow countrymen by reading over much of certain undesirable continentals whom they ape without understanding. But indifferentism to God the plain Anglo-Saxon must overcome. His neatly packaged, for emergency stored away in the corner God does not exist. The plain Anglo-Saxon must relearn that God is everywhere and should permeate everything—his state, his politics, his education, his books, his work, his play. The Portuguese shepherds of Fatima had God in their work and play, their food and shelter, their songs and dances. Christ is a part of their daily

culture. But in Anglo-Saxondom He is often only the forgotten reason of why one has a Sunday suit.

The American Anglo-Saxon with his well intentioned
separation of church and state has unfortunately secularized his entire existence. He is the supreme indifferentist
to God. And indifferentism, as the present Pope has so
well stressed, can be more injurious to the cause of God
than outright persecution. If the Anglo-Saxon American
wisely because of prevalent religious divisions separated
church and state, he must relearn that, in spite of his pru-
dent wisdom in the midst of religious division to give preference to no one religion at the expense of others, he nevertheless needs God in his state. He needs Him and His
principles everywhere. This need may not be so terribly
difficult for plain Anglo-Saxons to relearn, especially as
they stand under the threat of cosmic bombs in a world
divorced from Christ.

The Christian religious divisions in Anglo-Saxondom
are perhaps more seeming than real. In the center are
orthodox Protestants and Rome. They may take centuries
to fuse but they have very much in common, the Ten Commandments universally, and also very much of doctrine
and dogma, including in some groups even such matters
as the Sacraments and the Holy Trinity. They have a
tendency to call the same things bad—divorce, sins of the
flesh, intemperance, greed, injustice, tyranny, *etc.* In time
of stress they might quite easily emphasize what they have
in common against a common enemy, Bolshevism or
secularism, for example. On the religious periphery of
Anglo-Saxon Christendom are the secularist and "liberal"
Protestants and even some *soi-disant* Roman Catholics,
who individually under stress will fall in either direction,
either toward Christianity or away from it. They are very

dangerous to Anglo-Saxon Christendom because, including many of the pseudo-intellectuals, they have a tendency to call wrong right and right wrong. They support in many individual instances movements which superficially one would expect to find supported only in the extremes of totalitarianism and statism: euthanasia, the relativity of truth, birth control, selective breeding, and forced sterilization of almost anyone they in Nazi fashion designate to be undesirable according to their subjective criteria. They often constitute the self-appointed leaders of Anglo-Saxon policy and thought, but possibly because they are so universally available for self-appointed "leadership" they have less real following among the plain people with a healthy modicum of common sense than might superficially be dreaded. They are seemingly by the stress of our century being pushed farther and farther away from any remote contact with Christianity and probably will make common cause in many instances with the downright and shameless misleaders of the people, Communist or otherwise. In other instances they will probably be shocked back by the results of their thoughts and actions into making contact with the central bodies of Anglo-Saxon Christendom. The disappearance of such peripheral groups would probably do much to clarify the atmosphere and show the Anglo-Saxon world where Christ really lies. For false Christs can be confusing and that is essentially what many so-called Christian "liberals" in Anglo-Saxon lands are—men only a disgrace and a confusion to Christendom, false Christs. They can be unmasked as pure secularists, materialists, mechanists, totalitarians, indifferentists, atheists, agnostics, minions of Anti-Christ, and it is quite possible that our century can do the unmasking most effectively. Ours is a time when there is really no middle ground:

one is really for Christ or against Him. The plain Anglo-Saxon can perhaps almost as easily see this fact as can his brothers in Portugal or France or Germany or Switzerland or Belgium.

For ours is a Renaissance which does not belong solely to one country or continent but which will in due time embrace all the West. Each of us must encourage our spiritual *élans* into the future. We must not press back the drive of God, the awe before mystery, the uplift of the spirit into the infinite. We must not allow ourselves to dilute the mystery of religion by keeping of true religion only a few impotent social platitudes as much of Protestantism and non-orthodox Judaism are beginning to do. The religious future of the West is a Christian future. Christ was *both* God and man. We must not permit stress on one side of His nature—the human—to obliterate the more important truth that Christ, the Son of God, was first and foremost always God! "I am even before Abraham and the prophets were".

We must not be afraid of our New World of the Spirit, our new type of values. We must not be pessimistic nor over-optimistic. The full blossoming of the future is not immediately around the corner. The coming civilization of the Spirit was not established at the Moscow or Cairo or Teheran or Dumbarton Oaks or San Francisco or United Nations conferences, nor will it be made at Timbuctoo or around any possible mud puddle in the midst of the Gobi Desert. It will not be made at any mere political conference. It will not be made, or unmade, in the national elections or the form of government of any individual land, important as these may be. Elections and forms of government may have much to do with the building of the future, or they may have little or nothing. They may easily play the backward, materialistic "liberal", decadent rôles into which they so easily fall in in a century of vulgarity and decline. The future is not dependent on governments and it will not be permanently and impotently delayed by any array of blindlings in power, however universal they may be. The future, if need be, will come into being in spite of governments and in spite of blindlings as it has always done in the past wherever there was need. Nor has the future been established by the conclusion of the Second World War. The coming civilization of the Spirit, however, will not permanently fail.

We must be of good heart. We need have faith and strength and courage and service and Love of God. We must pray for His efficacious grace. We must cling not to the outmoded values built on superficial reality and on things and sensations, on materialism, and mechanism, on technological science and nihilistic liberalism. We must avoid doing our part to make the future infernal, hellish, chaotic. We must have faith in the justness and purpose of God. We must pray for His Mercy in our era of transition and for the grace to live through it bravely and creatively.

How can people everywhere be brought to realize the great and wonderful newness of our time? Is this so very difficult? Only time can answer. But seemingly there is much apparent reason to believe that Western man can learn that he must rebuild his world on Christ or else perish.

Our time, as we have seen, is not essentially different from that of a similar period in Rome. The same means by which Christianity was preached to the world then it must be preached again: by word of mouth, by books, by example, by Faith and Hope and Love of God. Our world stands in need of the same type of evangelization as Rome did in the time of Nero. Christ must be preached on the street corner, in shop, at work, and play, in Ireland and Portugal, in Italy and France, in Scotland and America. He must be preached not only by clergymen in churches but by clergymen wherever men congregate. And he must be preached by laymen. Laymen will be heard by many who would suspect a priest. Anti-clericals do not always mean to be anti-Christ, even if in practice they are usually so. But anti-clericals exist and laymen for certain purposes can be much more effective than clergymen in spreading the good news of Christ.

And Christ is good tidings. He is the best news that the world has ever had. He must be shouted from the house-tops, the classroom, the shop, the playground. Men must be compelled in from the high-ways and by-ways, even if at first they seem not to want to come. The banquet is ready. The Father is patiently waiting. The Gospel of Christ needs now to be carried by clerics and laymen alike to all their brothers whose faith is luke-warm or non-existent wherever their brothers may be. And it needs to be carried as it was in Rome at a similar period almost two thousand years ago, carried by the example of Christians, carried by book and pamphlet and magazine and newspaper, and above all carried by preachment of the Word of God wherever men are. The street corner preaching in London and Columbus Circle and Madrid, the traveling vans bringing the good tidings into the American Southland are the seeds out of which the New World will be born everywhere. Western man, plain folk and leaders too, needs to hear as never before about the Love of God and His infinite graces. Unto us a Savior is born! For what do the Incarnation, the Ministry and the

Crucifixion essentially mean? They mean that God has fulfilled His promise, His covenants. They mean that only man-made obstacles now lie in the way of building an adequate world. The infinite obstacle between man and God, the infinite insult of sin Christ God, Christ the Second Person of the Trinity, has removed. What man could never have done for himself Christ has done for him. He has taken upon Himself the infinite atonement for man's sins. Man is not capable of infinite atonement. He is capable of only finite things. God has now done His part. He leaves the rest up to man. The Incarnation and Crucifixion render an Infinite Challenge to man now to do his part. Christ God became man. He lived as man and laid down clear cut principles by whicn man can live to build the world aright. By His death he took upon Himself the satisfaction of the infinite obstacle between man and God, the infinite insult of sin. The Incarnation and Crucifixion do not remove the results of original sin. Man still has the clouded intellect, the weakened will, the penchant for evil. He is still the victim of concupiscence. But God and His Sacraments give man ready means by which to overcome evil. His Revelation is adequate for man to build a good world. Only finite and man-made obstacles remain. God has shown man what to do. He will help man do it, offers him an infinite treasury of graces. But it remains for man to implement his graces into action. God can help, but He cannot do everything and leave free will to man. God needs us to help Him. He needs our coöperation. He needs us to preach the mystery of the Incarnation, its meaning and challenge to man.

Man's only real enemy, only obstacle now is Satan, is the preference of Satan to God, a man-chosen preference, is sin. It is only the sins of men, the men-preferences of Satan to God, which now prevent man from building the most glorious civilization he has ever known. The great sorrow of our times is that so few really know the deep nature of the threat against us, the threat which is devastating the world. The real enemy is Satan himself who has poisoned nation against nation, race against race, group against group, man against man. And the cure against Satan is simple. It is Christ.

The hate and jealousy of Satan toward man is puny stuff compared with the love of God. Hate is rooted within and gets its strength only from the exhaustible inner will of evil. But the Love of God looks outward and embraces the universe. It is inexhaustible. The result is a battle of the exhaustible with the Inexhaustible, of the finite with the Infinite, of measurable hate with Immeasurable Love.

And the Love of God should be the chief emphasis in the preachment to our time, the Love of God for all men, and the necessity of their loving Him. Presbyterian may differ with Anglican and Lutheran with Catholic and Orthodox with Uniate, and these differences 'are serious before God. He sorrows for His one fold again in Christendom. But in our time we so terribly need to stress also what we have in common. And all of us emphasize the Love of God as surpassing all things. There abide only these Three, Faith, Hope, and Love of God. But the greatest of These is Love of God. Let Presbyterians, Baptists, Quakers, Anglicans, Uniates, Orthodox, and Catholics, and all other men of Good Will preach and live the Love of God. We have little to fear from the hate of Satan then. And *Deo volente* we can find through the preachment of the Love of God our Christian unity again.

Is it too much to ask of the plain folk of the West,

that they love God, listen to the preachment of the Love of God, and preach it to their brothers? It dare not be. The solution to the threat impending in our time is very simple. We need to be humble like little children. We need to be without self-seeking. We need to have Faith and Hope. We need above all else the Love of God.

And if the service of God is made in Western Christendom, what about Eastern Christendom? Here the problem is most complex of all, but again not hopeless. In the first place, under the crushing heel of Bolshevism in the enslaved countries there is the Faith of Rome in Poland, Hungary, Slovakia, Croatia, much of Bohemia and the Baltic lands, burning bright amidst persecution and horror. In the sister enslaved lands of Rumania, Serbia, Bulgaria there is Orthodox Christendom perhaps purified enough by suffering to throw off its ancient subservience to the state and speak out in its own right for the primacy of God. In doctrine and dogma it is so very close to Rome. It has the seven Sacraments of Christianity, the devotion to Mary and the saints, a valid clergy, an infinite treasury of God's grace. Even in the lands enslaved for decades, Muscovy, White Russia, Ukrainia there has not been eradicated the Love of God nor belief in Him nor devotion to His Blessed Mother. If the West sets the East a good example, in Faith, Hope, and Love of God, is it not almost an insult to God's grace to imagine that such an example would not find an answering echo among our fellow Christians of the East?

But even if the iron curtain could succeed—as it almost certainly could not—in shutting out a light radiant with the Love of God, have we not in the second place the hope of Fatima? All things are possible to God—and we can hope in miracles. The meaning of Fatima is clear. If the

West does its half of the miracle, if it repents and prays and loves God, Mary alone through her Immaculate Heart guarantees the rest. In this sense our fear need not be of Russia and the East. It need be only of our own indifference, our own sins, our own unrepentance, our own lack of the Love of God.

Thus, the New Renaissance of the Spirit depends on each of us, depends on our preachment of the Love of God, our Faith, our Hope, our works and prayers. It is not a matter for our neighbor only. It is a matter for us —to live each day as best we can, loving and honoring and serving God and doing His Will. Each of us is part of the leaven that must work until the whole is leavened. We may be few today. But if we cooperate with God's graces, we shall be trebled tomorrow, and legion in sufficient time to save the world from the threat of Satan which now impends. When the question is posed, "What can we do?", the answer is simple: kneel down and pray and then arise and act—by word, by preachment, by example for God! Not in self-seeking but in humility working for God we can build His Kingdom. With less attention on the mote in our brother's eye than on the tree in our own, we must stress God's Mercy and Grace and Love for all men regardless of race or color or social or political background. God loves even the sinner and is especially sorry for him because he has made such infinitely wrong and stupid choices, has exchanged Love for hate, Justice for injustice, Happiness for misery.

No one is excluded from God's plan except those who exclude themselves. He wants us all, capitalists, Communists, socialists, Fascists, proletarians, bourgeois, and princes, pagans, Jews, Protestants, Orthodox, Catholics, God wants us all and needs us all in His Kingdom and is sorry if we do not build it. He has in His Incarnation flung us the Infinite Challenge to do so. Our time must be the New Renaissance of the Spirit built each day by the works and prayers and Hope and Faith and Love of God in each of us.

The question must inevitably arise: what if our time should be Apocalyptic? It is futile to try to answer the question since not even the angels in Heaven are said to know the answer. It would be presumptuous, therefore, for man either to deny or to claim that our age may be an Apocalyptic one. Our responsibilities, however, in an Apocalyptic time remain the same in essense as they would in a non-apocalyptic age, are intensified only in degree. God is still with us, and any suffering entailed for us in upholding His Kingdom is necessary because we no longer have Purgatory to rely on so as by some narrow squeeze some day to get into Heaven.

If our time is Apocalyptic, then we are in the shadow of a New Renaissance of the Spirit dwarfing all other possible renaissances of revolving time. What we need to do in preaching and living the Love of God in a normal Renaissance would need to be done tenfold if we live under the gathering pestilence of the Beast. We need to be fortified ten fold in our zeal and in our Love, for the times will be so trying that God Himself assures us that no flesh could be saved unless He in His Mercy would shorten the days of horror. Yet, such suffering to introduce the universal Kingdom of Christ still should not make the steadfast Christian blanch with terror. He knows the rôle of suffering for its own sake in atonement for the injustice of man against God. He knows that the scales of justice must be balanced. It requires an incredible degree of spirituality to be like Ste. Thérèse of Lisieux and long to live in an Apocalyptic age: "My heart thrills at the thought of the frightful tortures Christians are to suffer at the time of the Anti-Christ and I long to undergo them all."[1] Yet, any steadfast Christian glimpses dimly what the Little Flower means by her ecstatic will to participate with Christ in the great atonement to bring the balances of God in equilibrium, no matter how much his flesh cringes and his weaker faith prays to be spared such complete testing. But the same stuff would be required to bring us into the Renaissance of the final millenium as into the Renaissance of the Spirit which this book has usually envisioned.

For an Apocalyptic age we need simply endlessly more the preachment and the living of the Love of God. We need endlessly more the emphases of Christ in our daily lives. We need endlessly more the representation of the Prince of Peace in our national and international policies, in our domestic and our foreign undertakings, in our philosophical and educational and economic and political systems. We need the works and prayers universally of all men of good will. And we need the intercession and help of Mary. She to whom power over the demons is granted gives us the final answer as to what to do in our time to usher in the New Renaissance of the Spirit. Whether the demons we have to overcome are the final ultimate, futile revolts of Satan against God, of the reign of the Beast, or whether they are only the very tangible and real and modern demons of materialism, mechanism, the superstitions of secularism and modernism and scientism, greed, self-seeking, and indifference to God, Mary His handmaid, gives up the model and the pattern for our actions to solve the difficulties of our time. Without self-seeking, in purity and humility, in Faith and Hope and

Love the New World can be born; and with the Grace and help of God and men there shall come into being over the horizon of our time a juster and a better world than man has ever known.

"Magnificat anima mea Dominum, et exultavit Spiritus meus in Deo salutari meo. Quia respexit humilitatem ancillae suae; ecce enim ex hoc beatam me dicent omnes generationes. Quia fecit mihi magna Qui potens est, et sanctum nomen Ejus. Et misericordia Ejus a progenie in progenies, timentibus Eum. Fecit potentiam in bracchio suo; dispersit superbos mente cordis sui. Deposuit potentes de sede, et exaltavit humiles. Esurientes implevit bonis: et divites dimisit inanes. Suscepit Israel puerum Suum; recordatus misericordiae Suae. Sicut locutus est ad patres nostros, Abraham, et semini ejus in saeculo."[2]

WHAT TO DO

Notes to Chapter Five

1. L'Histoire d'une Ame, Chapter XI.
2. Luke, I, 47-55.

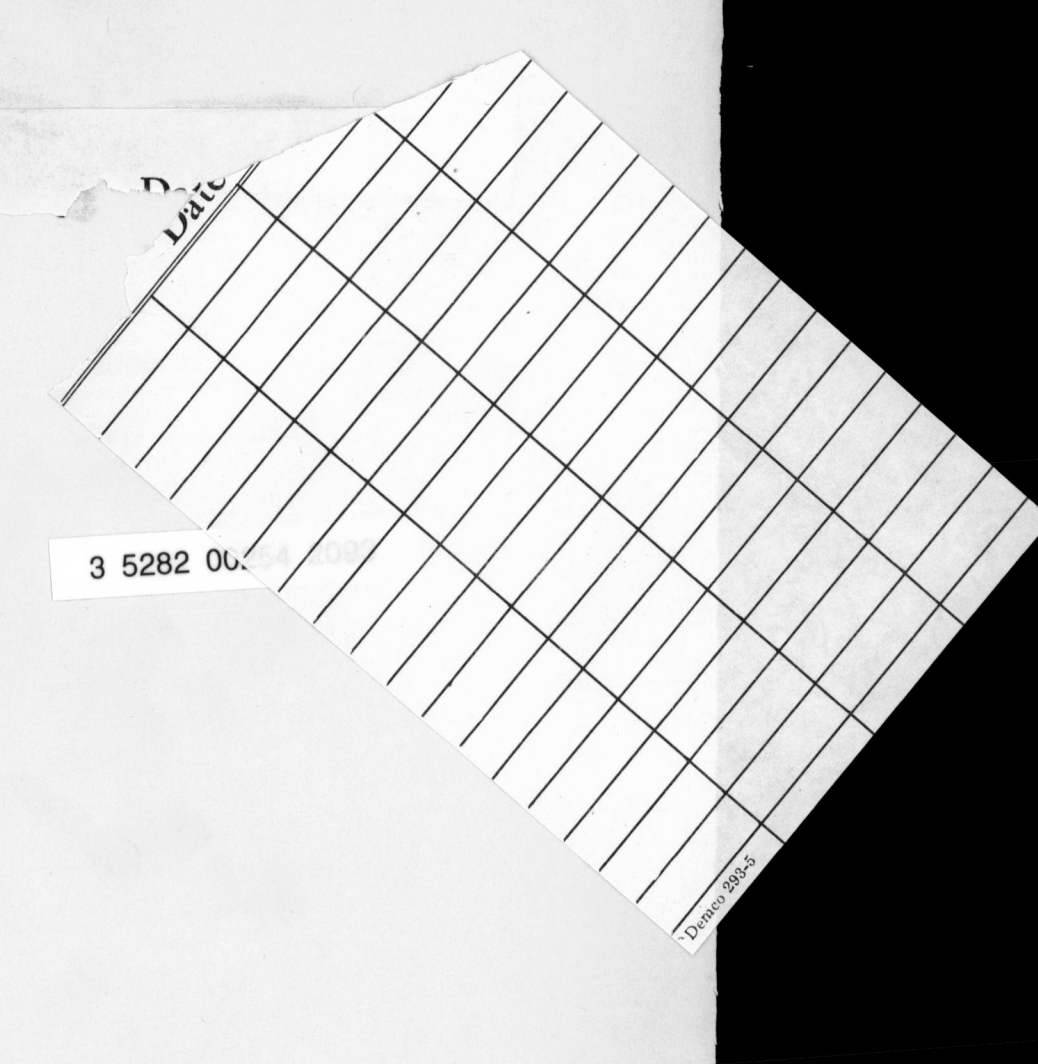

Demco 293-5